When Compressive Sensing Meets Mobile Crowdsensing

Linghe Kong · Bowen Wang ·
Guihai Chen

When Compressive Sensing Meets Mobile Crowdsensing

Springer

Linghe Kong
Department of Computer Science
and Engineering
Shanghai Jiao Tong University
Shanghai, China

Bowen Wang
ByteDance Ltd.
Beijing, China

Guihai Chen
Department of Computer Science
Nanjing University
Nanjing, China

ISBN 978-981-13-7778-5   ISBN 978-981-13-7776-1   (eBook)
https://doi.org/10.1007/978-981-13-7776-1

This Springer imprint is published by the registered company Springer Nature Singapore Pte Ltd.
The registered company address is: 152 Beach Road, #21-01/04 Gateway East, Singapore 189721,
Singapore

Preface

"I would recommend strongly this valuable and impactful monograph to researchers who are interested in the frontier of data management in mobile crowdsensing."

—*Prof. Laurence Tianruo Yang*
St Francis Xavier University, Canada
Fellow of the Canadian Academy of Engineering

"An valuable book brings together systematic Compressive Sensing with Mobile Crowdsensing and shows a promising possible future direction."

—*Prof. Meikang Qiu*
Columbia University, USA

"This monograph presents strategic insights for data quality challenge in mobile crowdsensing by leveraging compressive sensing. I would sincerely invite you to read and comment this book."

—*Prof. Jinjun Chen*
Swinburne University of Technology, Australia

Mobile crowdsensing, as an emerging sensing paradigm, enables the masses to join in data collection tasks using powerful mobile devices. However, date mobile crowdsensing platforms have yet to be widely adopted in practice. The major concern is the quality of the data collected by mobile crowdsensing. There are numerous causes: some locations may generate redundant data, while others may not be covered at all, since the participators are usually not systematically coordinated; privacy is a concern for some people, who don't wish to share their real-time locations, and therefore some key information may be missing; and some participants may upload fake data to fraudulently gain rewards. When compressive sensing meets mobile crowdsensing, these problematic aspects are gradually addressed.

This book provides a comprehensive introduction to applying compressive sensing to improve data quality in mobile crowdsensing. It covers the following topics: missing data reconstruction, fault data detection, data privacy preservation, multidimensional data conversion, and efficient task allocation.

Missing data is common in the mobile crowdsensing because the movements of participators are uncontrolled and some locations lack participators for sensing. From this book, readers can learn how to use the compressive sensing method to reconstruct the missing data, in which the essential compressive sensing is an effective solution to accurately recover a sparse signal using very few samples.

Faulty data is another data quality problem in mobile crowdsensing caused by unstable sensors and unreliable wireless transmissions. Especially, when missing data and faulty data coexist in practical crowdsensing, the problem becomes more intractable. To solve this problem, this book presents an extended compressive sensing method, namely iterative compressive sensing. By iteratively running compressive sensing and time series, the problem of missing value reconstruction and faulty data detection are decoupled.

In order to dispel participators' worry on privacy leakage, compressive sensing also shows its value. A homogeneous compressive sensing framework is introduced, which encrypts the data for privacy issues while maintaining the homomorphic obfuscation property for compressive sensing.

In some complicated mobile sensing scenarios, the collected data are multidimensional. The conventional compressive sensing cannot be directly utilized on such multidimensional data. This book introduces a converted compressive sensing method to convert the data structure, so that the compressive sensing can still be applied for data quality improvement.

Other than improving the quality of collected data, compressive sensing also facilitates the data collecting process in task allocation. We observe that more allocated tasks indicate higher data quality and higher cost in most mobile crowdsensing. Based on this observation, this book presents a compressive crowdsensing framework to reduce the cost by minimizing the number of allocated tasks, while guaranteeing the data quality.

Shanghai, China   Linghe Kong
April 2019   Bowen Wang
                                                                                              Guihai Chen

Acknowledgements

This book cannot be completed without the effort of many scholars, researchers, and engineers. Most of their names are not included by the authors. Here, we want to thank all the people who offered their help to this book. Specifically, we would like to express our gratitude to those who are willing to share their research results and give us permission to refer the data and graphs.

This book was also partially supported by the National Key R&D Program of China 2018YFB1004703, NSFC grant 61672349 and 61672353.

Shanghai, China
April 2019

Linghe Kong
Bowen Wang
Guihai Chen

Contents

Chapter 1
Introduction

Mobile Crowdsensing (MCS) [4, 11] is a promising paradigm that utilizes ubiquitous mobile devices to collect environmental data. However, mobile crowdsensing platforms have yet to be widely adopted in practice because of the data quality problems such as missing data, faulty data, and privacy issues. To deal with the data quality problems, this book introduces the compressive sensing method into mobile crowdsensing, where compressive sensing [2] is an effective method to accurately recover a sparse signal using very few samples. What will happen when compressive sensing meets mobile crowdsensing? You will find the results from this book. In this chapter, we will provide an overview of mobile crowdsensing and compressive sensing, and introduce the problem addressed in this book.

1.1 Mobile Crowdsensing Overview

The popularity of smartphones and other mobile devices (e.g., in-vehicle sensing devices such as GPS) enables the pervasive collection of a large volume of data. Mobile crowdsensing [4, 11] exploits such data collection opportunities by leveraging individuals to collect and share sensory data using their mobile devices. Furthermore, MCS is also a special and effective scheme for Internet of Things (IoT) [6, 9], which enables the environmental information to be collected and shared across platforms. Many MCS projects have emerged in recent years, including urban transportation monitoring [10], urban noise monitoring [1, 12], indoor floorplan construction [3, 13], and image sensing [7, 8].

Figure 1.1 shows the typical structure of mobile crowdsensing, which can be divided into three layers: data collection layer, data processing layer, and application layer. On the bottom is the data collection layer. This layer determines how to gather data using mobile devices. The data gathered from this layer are transferred to the data processing layer. In the data processing layer, the gathered data are processed and

© Springer Nature Singapore Pte Ltd. 2019
L. Kong et al., *When Compressive Sensing Meets Mobile Crowdsensing*, https://doi.org/10.1007/978-981-13-7776-1_1

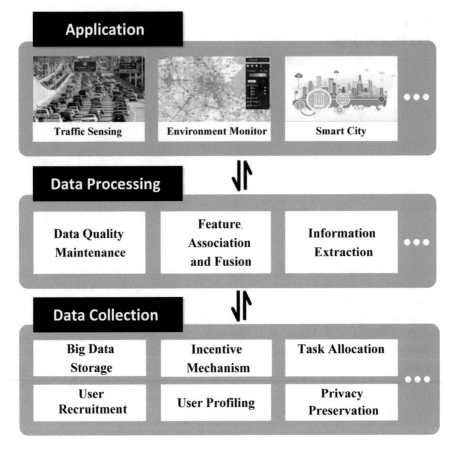

Fig. 1.1 Structure of mobile crowdsensing

analyzed, and useful information is extracted to support the dedicated applications such as traffic sensing, environment monitoring, and smart city. Next, we focus on the data collection layer and the data processing layer.

In the data collection layer, the MCS platform posts a series of sensing tasks according to the requirement of MCS requestors. For example, in urban noise monitoring system, the sensing tasks can be the noise collection in representative locations for a specific period or the urban-scale real-time traffic status. After the sensing tasks are created, the MCS platform then allocates them to appropriate participators to execute the tasks and upload the sensed data.

In the data processing layer, the gathered data are first preprocessed, in order to filter out invalid data and transform the data into an appropriate format for further analysis. Then, the preprocessed data are passed through data mining algorithms. The output can be a noise distribution graph for noise monitoring system, or the real-time traffic condition graph for traffic monitoring system.

As an emerging technology, piles of problems are waiting to be tackled. In this book, we focus on the following data quality problems:

- *Missing data and faulty data*: Due to the openness nature of mobile crowdsensing, it is difficult to guarantee the quality of collected data. Two common factors impact the data quality: missing data and faulty data.
- *Privacy preservation*: Privacy also significantly affects the data quality in mobile crowdsensing. Since the sensory data are provided by massive participators, these participators would not like to join the tasks if their privacy cannot be protected. Hence, the MCS system needs to guarantee the privacy to incent more participators to contribute.
- *Task allocation*: The movement of participators are uncontrolled. If the tasks can be allocated to appropriate participators, the quality of gathered data would be high and the cost would be low. Otherwise, the participators might lose the interest of task execution quickly.

How to address these problems? Let us first have a glance at a powerful tool: compressive sensing.

1.2 Compressive Sensing Overview

Compressive sensing (CS) [2] is a theory originally designed for compressing signals by represented vectors. The compressive sensing theory proves that if a signal is *sparse*, it can be sampled with a further lower rate than the classic Nyquist sampling rate [5]. Thus, the sparse signal can be compressed with a very high factor and reconstructed accurately. Compressive sensing has become a hotspot in the research community, as it has been rapidly and successfully applied to electrical engineering, communication, statistics, machine learning, image processing, sensor network, and many other fields.

In mobile crowdsensing, the problems mentioned in Sect. 1.1 are all directly or indirectly related to data sampling. Compressive sensing is potential to facilitate these problems.

1.3 Organization

In this book, we will see how compressive sensing helps to tackle the data quality challenges in mobile crowdsensing. The rest of this book is organized as follows: In Chaps. 2 and 3, we introduce the basic knowledge of mobile crowdsensing and compressive sensing, respectively. Chapters 4 and 5 address the data quality maintenance problem. Among them, Chap. 4 focuses on missing data, while Chap. 5 further takes faulty data into consideration. Chapter 6 shows how compressive sensing preserves the data privacy. In Chap. 7, we present how to apply compressive sensing into the complicated multidimensional data in mobile crowdsensing. Chapter 8 presents the concept of *compressive crowdsensing* and shows how compressive sensing reduces the cost of data collection while guaranteeing the data quality. Finally, we conclude this book in Chap. 9.

In each chapter from Chap. 4 to Chap. 8, first, readers can understand the background of the topic. Next, readers can learn how to formally define the problem and interpret the rationale of the compressive sensing based approach. Then, readers can find the performance evaluations of compressive sensing-based solutions in simulation or experiment.

References

1. Bello JP, Silva C, Nov O, DuBois RL, Arora A, Salamon J, Mydlarz C, Doraiswamy H (2018) SONYC: a system for the monitoring, analysis and mitigation of urban noise pollution. arXiv:180500889
2. Donoho DL (2006) Compressed sensing. Trans Inf Theory (TIT) 52(4):1289–1306
3. Elhamshary M, Youssef M, Uchiyama A, Yamaguchi H, Higashino T (2016) Transitlabel: a crowd-sensing system for automatic labeling of transit stations semantics. In: The international conference on mobile systems, applications, and services (Mobisys). ACM, pp 193–206
4. Ganti RK, Ye F, Lei H (2011) Mobile crowdsensing: current state and future challenges. Commun Mag 49(11)
5. Jerri AJ (1977) The shannon sampling theorem-its various extensions and applications: a tutorial review. Proc IEEE 65(11):1565–1596
6. Liu J, Shen H, Narman HS, Chung W, Lin Z (2018) A survey of mobile crowdsensing techniques: a critical component for the internet of things. ACM Trans Cyber-Phys Syst (TCPS) 2(3):18
7. Mao W, Wang M, Qiu L (2018) Aim: acoustic imaging on a mobile. In: International conference on mobile systems, applications, and services (MobiSys). ACM, pp 468–481
8. Wu Y, Wang Y, Hu W, Cao G (2016) Smartphoto: a resource-aware crowdsourcing approach for image sensing with smartphones. Trans Mob Comput (TMC) 15(5):1249–1263
9. Xia F, Yang LT, Wang L, Vinel A (2012) Internet of things. Int J Commun Syst 25(9):1101
10. Yoon J, Noble B, Liu M (2007) Surface street traffic estimation. In: The international conference on mobile systems, applications, and services (Mobisys). ACM, pp 220–232
11. Zhang D, Wang L, Xiong H, Guo B (2014) 4w1h in mobile crowd sensing. Commun Mag 52(8):42–48
12. Zheng Y, Liu T, Wang Y, Zhu Y, Liu Y, Chang E (2014) Diagnosing New York city's noises with ubiquitous data. In: International joint conference on pervasive and ubiquitous computing (UbiComp). ACM, pp 715–725
13. Zhou R, Lu X, Zhao HS, Fu Y, Tang MJ (2019) Automatic construction of floor plan with smartphone sensors. J Electron Sci Technol 17(1):13–25

Chapter 2
Mobile Crowdsensing

Supported by the large quantity of mobile devices embedded with rich sensors, Mobile Crowdsensing (MCS) leverages these devices to sense and contribute data in order to extract intelligence and provide corresponding services. Since most MCS applications rely on high-quality sensing data, plenty of quality-aware incentive mechanisms, authentications mechanisms, preprocessing algorithms, or outlier detection on sensed data are proposed for quality management in MCS projects. In this chapter, we will introduce the data quality problem in MCS, together with existing solutions except compressive sensing.

2.1 Background

Mobile devices nowadays have been equipped with various sensors including accelerometers, gyroscopes, cameras, and so on. According to the statistics of the International Telecommunications Union (ITU) in 2018 [1], global mobile cellular telephone subscriptions have grown more than 30% in the last 5 years. Furthermore, there are even more mobile cellular subscriptions than people on the planet, where every 100 inhabitants have around 110 subscriptions [1]. Inspired by such popularity of mobile devices, MCS is proposed [14] to realize more flexible and efficient data acquisition, analysis, and application than fixed Wireless Sensor Networks (WSN). The formal definition of MCS can be expressed as [16]:

> Mobile crowdsensing is a new sensing paradigm that empowers ordinary citizens to contribute data sensed or generated from their mobile devices, aggregates and fuses the data in the cloud for crowd intelligence extraction and human-centric service delivery.

The typical MCS scheme consists of three main components: participators (or users), platform, and requestors, while in some scenarios, the participators and requestors are the same entity (e.g., the requestors can also go to collect data).

© Springer Nature Singapore Pte Ltd. 2019
L. Kong et al., *When Compressive Sensing Meets Mobile Crowdsensing*, https://doi.org/10.1007/978-981-13-7776-1_2

Requestors will initiate sensing requests and provide corresponding constraints including budgets and coverage requirements forwarded to the MCS platform. The platform side is responsible for assigning tasks and publishing rewards to a suitable subset of mobile device users, with the consideration of constraints. Participators will upload the sensed data after accepting their sensing tasks, which will be collected, stored, and processed by the MCS platform and is finally returned to requestors. This collaborative scheme builds the connection between industries, governments, organizations, and ordinary people, which plays an important role in supporting sustainable development goals, including economic, social, and environmental requirements [46].

As its name implies, MCS has three main characteristics in this typical scheme:

- **"Mobile"**: The participators and devices are in moving status subjectively, so the coverage of participators and the quality of sensing data are required to be controlled.
- **"Crowd"**: The large group of individuals having mobile devices are capable of participating in the sensing projects. But different trajectories or preferences of participators will lead to the data heterogeneity, such as the uneven distribution of sensing data.
- **"Sensing"**: Participators are mostly required to execute some simple sensing tasks without massive computations.

As mentioned in Chap. 1, three data-oriented layers are summarized in a complete MCS system: data collection layer, data processing layer, and application layer. For a better intelligence extraction and application, high-quality data are needed in every stage of MCS. For example, *In the data collection layer*, participator recruitment, selection, and identification guarantee the collection capability. *In the data processing layer*, the preprocessing and post-processing including outlier detection and data correction can be considered for data quality management. In the following sections, we will discuss the data quality problem in MCS and possible solutions in detail.

2.2 Data Quality Problem in Mobile Crowdsensing

Due to the openness of mobile crowdsensing, the data quality problem has to be concerned in its design. For example, outright device malfunction, transmission error, or low sensory accuracy caused by environmental issues (e.g., mobile phone kept in a pocket while sampling the street-level noise) [53]; fake or invalid data from malicious users [35]; uneven distribution of sensing locations; and so on.

Figure 2.1 shows existing data quality solutions in the typical mobile crowdsensing scheme, which improves the data quality from various directions. The modern sensors can achieve high sensory accuracy [18]. Incentive mechanisms are specially designed to avoid malicious activities when encouraging more participators. After enough participator recruitment, the participator groups can be classified according to quality evaluation. The participator, who has stronger sensing capability, has higher possibility to execute sensing tasks. Furthermore, the identification of selected participators should be authenticated to avoid malicious participators. After rich sensing data collection, lightweight preprocessing strategies can be applied on the edge. The left erroneous data can be finally fixed by outlier detection or correctness strategies. Next, we classify existing data quality solutions into six categories and discuss them in detail.

2.3 Existing Data Quality Solutions in Mobile Crowdsensing

To guarantee the high-quality sensing in mobile crowdsensing for further applications, many excellent solutions have been proposed. As illustrated in Fig. 2.1, we classify them into quality-aware incentive mechanisms, quality-driven participator selection mechanisms, authentication mechanisms, quality-driven task allocation mechanisms, lightweight preprocessing strategies, and outlier detection and data correction.

2.3.1 Quality-Aware Incentive Mechanisms

The data quality in incentive mechanisms is evaluated by the trustworthiness of participators according to their sensed data. Two kinds of incentive mechanisms: game and auction, both have data quality-aware incentive instantiations.

As for **game-based incentive mechanisms**, the Trustworthy Sensing for Crowd Management (TSCM) model [22] enhances the Stackelberg Game by introducing reputation awareness and trustworthiness of participators. An outlier detection algorithm [53] proposed accordingly is used to detect possibly altered data which directly affects the trustworthiness of the corresponding participator.

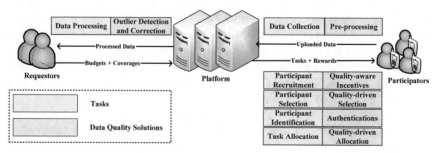

Fig. 2.1 The illustration of the relationship between data quality solutions and tasks in typical mobile crowdsensing scheme

In the equilibrium-based game, participators join a subset of this game whose strategies follow the Nash equilibrium (NE). Participators can optionally decide to vote *accept* or *refuse* for a sensing task [34]. To keep a high data quality of contributed data, the reputation of each participator will be evaluated by their voting capacity. This capacity will be increased only when the dissimilarity between uploading and uploaded data is above a certain threshold, efficiently avoiding redundant data collection. Correspondingly, the rewards to voters will increase when their data dissimilarity is larger, or decrease vice versa. As the reward system is tightly bounded with the reputation of voters, this game can efficiently promote the trustworthiness of participators.

As for **auction-based incentive mechanisms**, data quality-aware mechanisms should pay as how well the participators do [33]. Multi-attributive Auction (MAA) mechanisms [2, 25] combine multiple attributes to evaluate the data quality. They select the sensing data of the highest data quality and give users corresponding incentives. Not only the multi-attributive data but also the multi-attributive users should be considered to get high-quality results, like Reputation-based Incentives for Data Dissemination (RIDD) [26] and Cheating-Resilient Incentive (CRI) [54]. As the trustworthiness of data is directly related to users' reputations, Pouryazdan et al. [36] propose an anchor-assisted and vote-based incentive mechanism. Before recruitment, the controller selects some anchor points who have 100% trustworthiness during a predefined time period. The trustworthiness of every node will be voted by any other node where the anchor node has the full capacity on voting.

Instead of the multi-attributive character, Koutsopoulos et al. [23] propose an optimal reverse auction with multiple winners based on Vickery–Clark–Groves (VCG) auction [4]. This method utilizes the incentive compatible mechanism. The strategies where each user reports its true cost follow the Bayesian NE. This auction scheme is a type of the second price auction for multiple items. Any user tends to give a high bidding to win, but it can not win at all. Actually, the winning cost of this user depends on the second user's bid, so such a high bidding price will also increase others' social costs. Only when the user's bidding price is equal to the true value of an object, this user can finally win.

Similarly, Jin et al. [21] incorporate the data quality to design an incentive mechanism based on the reverse combinatorial auctions. Here, the users can bid on the combination of different kinds of commodities. This paper not only studies the single-minded scenario where every user is willing to execute one subset of tasks, but also investigates the multi-minded cases in which any user might be interested in executing multiple subsets of tasks. Since the winner determination in this auction is an NP-hard problem, this paper designs a computationally efficient mechanism with the close-to-optimal social welfare.

Further enhanced, Sun et al. [40] propose a behavior-based incentive mechanism with budget constraints by applying sequential all-pay auctions. All participators have to pay their irrevocable bids and fulfill the bids regardless of who the winner is [29]. This mechanism incorporates a winning probability into the utility function and thereby makes the all-pay equivalent to winner-pay auctions [30]. In this auction scheme, all competitors will try their best to win the bid, which can improve the data quality and promote continuous participation.

However, all of the auctions mentioned above depend on the full participation of sensing tasks. But in practice, the sensing time of users is limited depending on their daily schedules. Motivated by this concern, Duan et al. [11] propose a Time schedule-Preferred Auction Scheme (TPAS), considering the partial fulfillment, attributive diversity, and price diversity. For instance, the partial fulfillment means the sensing tasks require the sensing time from 9:00 pm to 11:00 pm, but the user can only sense from 10:00 pm to 10:30 pm. The attributive diversity represents different sensing abilities for users like the quality of their sensors and their initial locations. And the price diversity is the different requirement on rewards varied by users. The TPAS follows the first-come-first-serve principle and greedily chooses the potential winner until no task or candidate can be selected. The final evaluations prove its computationally efficient, individually rational, budget balanced, and truthful performances.

2.3.2 Quality-Driven Participator Selection Mechanisms

Intuitively, the evaluation on equipped devices for participators can indicate their qualifications, which affects their hard reputation for their sensed data quality, including the battery, network bandwidth, sensor state, number of sensors, and rated sensor powers [6].

Similar to the Sociability-Oriented and Battery-Efficient Recruitment (SOBER) [3], Fiandrino et al. [13] design a participant recruitment strategy named DSE. "D" inside is *Distance*, representing the distance between the candidate and sensing task location; "S" is *Sociability*, implying the willingness of a candidate the participate in sensing tasks; and "E" is *Energy*, concerning about the remaining battery of the mobile device. To evaluate the quality of candidate i, her recruitment factor R_i is calculated by the weighted sum of D, S, and E, where the weight of each factor is application-dependent. As the sum of these three parameters equals unity, each higher value implies the preference of certain recruitment strategy. Finally, only the recruitment factor R which is above the threshold will be considered and the highest several Rs will be selected until reaching the budget constraint.

Song et al. [39] dynamically select a minimum subset of participants to provide the best data quality satisfaction metrics for all tasks. Although it still uses the greedy algorithm, the selection criteria of this paper are comprehensive, including the expected amount of collected data, the required data quality, and users' reward expectations. In this method, the data quality metrics are calculated by data granularity and quantity. For example, the sensing tasks require the amount of data as $(3, 3, 2, 1)$ in four areas, respectively, and there are three participants (a, b, c). If we choose (a, b), they have abilities to assembly collect $(3, 2, 2, 1)$ in these areas, while if we choose (b, c), the collect result is $(3, 3, 1, 0)$. Although (b, c) finish the former two tasks, they collect less data in the latter two tasks. Compared with them, (a, b) finish tasks more balanced and efficient. Mathematically, the authors calculate the ratio between the required metrics and the collected metrics to define this data quality. They declare that the data quality of (a, b) is higher than (b, c).

What's more, Wang et al. [44] take reputation values of participants into consideration. Two attributes are needed to define this reputation value: participation willingness and data quality. Inspired by the social principle, willingness is calculated by the average time gap between two collected behaviors. The shorter the time gap is, the more enthusiastic the participator will be. So, the feedback value for each participator can be represented by the combination of this calculated willingness, data quality, and rewards. After participators contribute sensing data to the platform, their reputation values will be monitored by watchdog and updated dynamically according to this feedback.

Although the PSP problem is considered similar to the knapsack problem, the uncertainty of sensing values and quality make it more challenging than the knapsack problem. To minimize the difference between the achieved total sensing revenue and the optimal one, Han et al. [17] give an online learning algorithm based on the Multi-Armed Bandit (MAB) paradigm [7] to acquire the statistical information on sensing values and qualities during the participation selection process. However, the lack of ground truth data leads to the failure of data quality estimation. To solve this problem, a context-aware data quality estimation scheme is proposed [27]. Depending on the historical sensing data, a context-quality classifier indicates the relationship between the context information of participators (i.e., keeping still, walking, or running) and their sensing data quality. Some volunteers like the running ones (have low sensing quality in noise sensing) will be filtered out by this context recognition rather than data quality estimation.

As the abovementioned strategies are all considering individual-based selection, Azzam et al. [5] design a Group-based Recruitment System (GRS) to assess the data quality in a group of participators collectively. The data quality of each group will be represented by their own fitness value, including the coverage of sensing tasks, members' distributions, device availability, the reputation of participators, sampling frequency, residual energy, and group cost. A mutate algorithm is applied to select the most fit groups until occurring the convergence, where maximal data quality remains unchanged after several iterations.

2.3.3 Authentication Mechanisms

Malicious false attack in MCS is easily ignored but devastating. On the one hand, some mischievous or malicious users seek to fool the system by falsifying data reporting. On the other hand, adversaries will pretend to be the normal user and report a flood of copies to overload crowdsensing applications (i.e., DoS attack), who are called Sybil devices. So, the proper authentication is needed to against this attack, to avoid such fake participators (i.e., programs or virtual machines). As the first firewall in data quality management, various authentication methods have been applied in current MCS systems, including slider dragging, verification code inputting, categorized photo selecting, etc. Similar with the Amazon Turk's login system, some direct questions like "what is the name of this project?" can also work well for simple identity authentication [15]. A real user can quickly give the right answer, while a program will fail without specific coding. Additionally, three enhanced authentications are discussed followingly: grid detection, DOS-resistant authentications, and colocation edges authentications.

Grid detection: Fatemieh et al. [12] regard the area of interest as a grid of square cells. This proposed mechanism is based on identifying outlier measurements inside of these cells, as well as corroboration among neighboring cells in a hierarchical structure to find out malicious nodes.

Consider a cell C_j containing m nodes and a dispute threshold for this cell d_0, which is the maximum acceptable difference between the measurements of two nodes in that cell. Assuming that each pairwise comparison nodes are N_i and N_j, if the difference is greater than d_0, the dispute counts c_i and c_j for N_i and N_j, respectively, are increased by one. After all pairwise comparisons, if $\frac{c_i}{m}$ is greater than or equal to the outlier threshold, the node is flagged as an outlier.

DOS-resistant authentications: Due to the openness of the MCS system, the malicious attack is likely to generate task abortion by giving Denial of Service (DoS) attack. As the improvement of Multi-level Timed Efficient Stream Loss-tolerant Authentication (μTESLA), Ruan at al. [37] formulate the attack-defense model as an evolutionary game, and then presents an optimal solution, which achieves security assurance along with minimum resource cost.

This method first sets multiple buffers for nodes and randomly selects packages stored in node buffers. Second, Message Authentication Codes (MACs) are broadcasted, and then μMACs calculated with a hash function, are stored in nodes. Finally, after the key is disclosed, the message will be sent and the receiver can use this disclosed key to compute the theoretical MAC of the received packet. After comparing it with its attached MAC, the received packets are authenticated.

Colocation edges authentication: Wang et al. [43] intend to defend against Sybil devices based on colocation edges. These edges are the authenticated records that attest to the one-time physical colocation of a pair of devices. As Sybil devices cannot physically interact with real devices, the edges between them and the rest of the network cannot be formed. Based on this, the problem of detecting ghost riders is simplified as a detection problem on the proximity graph. As a detail, after creating the colocation edges graph, SybilRank [8] algorithm first computes the landing probability for short random walks from trusted nodes to land on all other nodes. Then normalized by the nodes' degrees, it calculates their landing probabilities as the trust scores for ranking. As short random walks from trusted nodes are very unlikely to traverse the few attack edges to reach Sybil nodes, the ranking scores of Sybil devices will be lower. So, a cutoff threshold can be set on the trust score, and the tail of the ranked list is labeled as Sybil devices. According to its simulation results, the cost for Sybil attacks to break its defense is tremendous, illustrating the feasibility of this method.

2.3.4   Quality-Driven Task Allocation Mechanisms

The sensed data quality will be considered as the contribution of each participator in task allocation mechanisms. Dynamic mechanisms widely apply this indicator to allocate suitable tasks to the most efficient group of people.

Xiong et al. [48, 49] propose a dynamic task assignment strategy to ensure the full coverage of the target area. The current states of the candidates can are evaluated and the corresponding tasks are assigned to the candidates. The following three states are considered: (i) If a participator has not called the first time, she will receive her task information; (ii) If a participator has finished her first call, she is required to upload his data at her next call; (iii) If a participator has finished two calls in a sensing cycle, she will not be assigned in this cycle. During the iteration of this assignment, the performances of candidates are assessed according to their contribution and the task will be dynamically assigned to the most suitable participator in the future round. And this iteration will stop, until the received data reaches the predefined amount or the sensing areas is fully covered.

Another distributed framework [9] lets each device compute their data collection utility, sensing potential, and environmental context to comprehensively determine whether to take the sensing tasks. The data collection utility depends on the amount of already-collected data in certain sensing area, which is feedback by cloud collectors [10]. The higher requirement for further uploading leads to a larger value of this parameter. The sensing potential is represented by the local energy consumption for mobile devices to sense and upload sensing data. And the environmental context circumstances the status of the mobile device, such as the location or the mobility pattern [50].

2.3.5   Lightweight Preprocessing Strategies

These strategies aim to improve the quality of uploaded data by preprocessing on the sensed data, where only satisfied data can be selected for transmission. To be efficiently applied in mobile devices, this system should be lightweight, where few computational resources are required in its processing. A lightweight comprehensive validation system optimizes and integrates several evaluation operations in one algorithm [24]: clustering, classification, change detection, and frequent patterns analysis. This algorithm is also robust for different types of devices, where parameters related to battery level, CPU usage level, data stream rate, and other systematical settings can be customized.

AI techniques are widely used in MCS data anlaysis. Limited by the computational capability of edge devices, lightweight AI models should be compressed for efficient running. Two main model compression techniques are researched recently. For the single-model compression, the cache-based convolutional optimization and tensor decomposition in DeepMon [28] can decrease the computational complexity of models. DeepEye [31] leverages the memory caching and SVD-based model compression to support multi-model running. And MobileNet [20] proposes a depth-wise separable convolution, combined by a single-filter derived convolution and 1*1 pointwise convolution. However, their targeting devices are supported by quite powerful CPU and GPU processors (e.g., 2GHz), which is not directly suitable for commodity surveillance cameras. Additionally, for the joint model compression, teacher–student strategy [19, 55] is famous for its good performance, where the student light network will be deployed on devices for preprocessing on sensed data.

2.3.6 Outlier Detection and Data Correction

Both the detection of faulty data (also called as truth discovery [32] or outlier detection [42]), and the correction on them can help to improve the quality of collected data.

As for the detection, the comparison between the collected data and the ground truth can detect redundant or missing data. Take photo quality estimation as an example, some high-quality photos on certain areas can be downloaded online and the comparison is made to filter redundant and irrelevant photos. A straightforward comparison method is to apply computer vision techniques where the target will be recognized in photos (i.e., to evaluate relevance) and the similarity between two photos should be lower than the threshold (i.e., to detect redundancy) [38, 45, 52]. However, the large cost to run these machine learning models including time consumption on model training, the CPU and GPU operation consumption, and the bandwidth occupation to transmit full pictures or download ground truth cannot be neglected. To solve this problem, Wu et al. [47] develop a resource-friendly photo coverage model to quantify the value of photos. Only the metadata of photos is analyzed to infer their coverage to target areas and corresponding quality values. These metadata include locations, orientations, and views of the camera, which will be caught by GPS, accelerometers, and magnetic field sensors in mobile devices. Consider them as just a series of floating numbers, then the transmission, computation, and storage process can all be lightweight and cost-efficient.

Another observation used in comparison is the similarity of collected data between neighboring areas or during a short-term spatially and temporarily. For example, the weather among subareas in a district will be similar, and the prices for goods in one supermarket will also be similar during a short period. Taking this observation into consideration, Zhang et al. [51] leverage graph comparison on historical human traces to correct the obvious numerical errors and detect missing records. After comparing the data collected in a short time, the authors can filter out the duplicated records. Advanced in technology, Talasila et al. [41] require both collected photos and correlated Bluetooth scan results to reveal the device's belonging Bluetooth communication area. First, the framework manually or automatically validates some photos' trustworthiness. This step can be operated by human eyes or graphics recognition algorithm, which takes the ground truth photos collected by trusted experimenters as a baseline. The locations and time of these validated photos will be the referenced data to extend verification with nearby collected point results in the same time. Here, the Bluetooth scan results are used to justify "nearby" data. After analyzing the location of the photo, if it is in the referenced area, it is considered to be true.

This observation is further applied in an optimization-based truth discovery problem where the ground truth for comparison is unknown [32]. The correlation between entities divides the whole group of data into different independent sets, where the correlated data gather in the same cluster. An objective function is applied to each cluster to measure the difference between the collected data and its unknown truth, adding the reliability of participators as its unknown weights. The ground truth will be estimated and updated depending on the optimization of this function and the correlation regularization terms will punish the deviations in the truths between correlated entities, until satisfying the coverage criteria.

2.4   Summary

In this chapter, we first introduce the basic concept of mobile crowdsensing, together with its typical scheme and characteristics. We further discuss the data quality problem in mobile crowdsensing. To address the data quality problem, existing solutions are presented in different categories. These solutions are individually excellent, but their fundamental sources are different. Thus, their combinations exist compatibility problem. On the contrary, this book will introduce the systematic solution based on the same foundation: compressive sensing.

References

1. (2017) Ict facts and figures 2017. https://www.itu.int/en/ITU-D/Statistics/Pages/facts/default.aspx
2. Albers A, Krontiris I, Sonehara N, Echizen I (2017) Coupons as monetary incentives in participatory sensing. Ifip Adv Inf Commun Technol 399:226–237
3. Anjomshoa F, Kantarci B (2018) SOBER-MCS: sociability-oriented and battery efficient recruitment for mobile crowd-sensing. Sensors 18(5):1593
4. Ausubel LM, Milgrom P et al (2006) The lovely but lonely vickrey auction. Comb Auction 17:22–26
5. Azzam R, Mizouni R, Otrok H, Ouali A, Singh S (2016) Grs: a group-based recruitment system for mobile crowd sensing. J Netw Comput Appl 72:38–50
6. Bajaj G, Singh P (2018) Load-balanced task allocation for improved system lifetime in mobile crowdsensing. In: IEEE MDM, Aalborg, Denmark
7. Bubeck S, Cesa-Bianchi N (2012) Regret analysis of stochastic and nonstochastic multi-armed bandit problems. Found Trends Mach Learn 5(1):101–112
8. Cao Q, Sirivianos M, Yang X, Pregueiro T (2012) Aiding the detection of fake accounts in large scale social online services. In: USENIX NSDI, San Jose, CA, USA

9. Capponi A, Fiandrino C, Kliazovich D, Bouvry P (2017a) Energy efficient data collection in opportunistic mobile crowdsensing architectures for smart cities. In: IEEE INFOCOM WKSHPS, Atlanta, GA

10. Capponi A, Fiandrino C, Kliazovich D, Bouvry P, Giordano S (2017b) A cost-effective distributed framework for data collection in cloud-based mobile crowd sensing architectures. IEEE Trans Sustain Comput 2(1):3–16

11. Duan Z, Li W, Cai Z (2017) Distributed auctions for task assignment and scheduling in mobile crowdsensing systems. In: IEEE ICDCS, Atlanta, GA, USA

12. Fatemieh O, Chandra R, Gunter CA (2010) Secure collaborative sensing for crowd sourcing spectrum data in white space networks. In: IEEE DySPAN, Singapore

13. Fiandrino C, Anjomshoa F, Kantarci B, Kliazovich D, Bouvry P, Matthews JN (2017) Sociability-driven framework for data acquisition in mobile crowdsensing over fog computing platforms for smart cities. IEEE Trans Sustain Comput 2(4):345–358

14. Ganti RK, Ye F, Lei H (2011) Mobile crowdsensing: current state and future challenges. IEEE Commun Mag 49(11):32–39

15. Goncalves J, Ferreira D, Hosio S, Liu Y, Rogstadius J, Kukka H, Kostakos V (2013) Crowdsourcing on the spot: altruistic use of public displays, feasibility, performance, and behaviours. In: ACM UbiComp, Zurich, Switzerland

16. Guo B, Wang Z, Yu Z, Wang Y, Yen NY, Huang R, Zhou X (2015) Mobile crowd sensing and computing: the review of an emerging human-powered sensing paradigm. ACM Comput Surv 48(1):7:1–7:31

17. Han K, Zhang C, Luo J (2016) Taming the uncertainty: budget limited robust crowdsensing through online learning. IEEE/ACM Trans Netw 24(3):1462–1475

18. He Y, Li Y (2013) Physical activity recognition utilizing the built-in kinematic sensors of a smartphone. IJDSN 9

19. Hinton GE, Vinyals O, Dean J (2015) Distilling the knowledge in a neural network. arXiv:CoRR/abs/1503.02531

20. Howard AG, Zhu M, Chen B, Kalenichenko D, Wang W, Weyand T, Andreetto M, Adam H (2017) Mobilenets: efficient convolutional neural networks for mobile vision applications. arXiv:CoRR/abs/1704.04861

21. Jin H, Su L, Chen D, Nahrstedt K, Xu J (2015) Quality of information aware incentive mechanisms for mobile crowd sensing systems. In: ACM MobiHoc, Hangzhou, China

22. Kantarci B, Mouftah HT (2014) Trustworthy sensing for public safety in cloud-centric internet of things. Internet Things J IEEE 1(4):360–368

23. Koutsopoulos I (2013) Optimal incentive-driven design of participatory sensing systems. In: IEEE INFOCOM, Turin, Italy

24. Krishnaswamy S, Gama J, Gaber MM (2012) Mobile data stream mining: from algorithms to applications. In: IEEE MDM, Bengaluru, India

25. Krontiris I, Albers A (2012) Monetary incentives in participatory sensing using multi-attributive auctions. Int J Parallel Emergent Distrib Syst 27(4):317–336

26. Li J, Wang X, Yu R, Liu R (2015) Reputation-based incentives for data dissemination in mobile participatory sensing networks. Int J Distrib Sens Netw 2015:1–13

27. Liu S, Zheng Z, Wu F, Tang S, Chen G (2017) Context-aware data quality estimation in mobile crowdsensing. In: IEEE INFOCOM, Atlanta, GA, USA

28. Loc HN, Lee Y, Balan RK (2017) Deepmon: mobile gpu-based deep learning framework for continuous vision applications. MobiSys. Niagara Falls, NY, USA, pp 82–95

29. Luo T, Tan HP, Xia L (2014) Profit-maximizing incentive for participatory sensing. In: IEEE INFOCOM, Toronto, Canada

30. Luo T, Kanhere SS, Huang J, Das SK, Wu F (2017) Sustainable incentives for mobile crowdsensing: Auctions, lotteries, and trust and reputation systems. IEEE Commun Mag 55(3):68–74

31. Mathur A, Lane ND, Bhattacharya S, Boran A, Forlivesi C, Kawsar F (2017) Deepeye: resource efficient local execution of multiple deep vision models using wearable commodity hardware. MobiSys. Niagara Falls, NY, USA, pp 68–81

32. Meng C, Jiang W, Li Y, Gao J, Su L, Ding H, Cheng Y (2015) Truth discovery on crowd sensing of correlated entities. In: ACM Sensys, Seoul, South Korea
33. Peng D, Wu F, Chen G (2015) Pay as how well you do: a quality based incentive mechanism for crowdsensing. In: IEEE SECON, Seattle, WA, USA
34. Pouryazdan M, Fiandrino C, Kantarci B, Soyata T, Kliazovich D, Bouvry P (2017a) Intelligent gaming for mobile crowd-sensing participants to acquire trustworthy big data in the internet of things. IEEE Access 5(99):22209–22223
35. Pouryazdan M, Kantarci B, Soyata T, Foschini L, Song H (2017b) Quantifying user reputation scores, data trustworthiness, and user incentives in mobile crowd-sensing. IEEE Access 5(99):1382–1397
36. Pouryazdan M, Kantarci B, Soyata T, Song H (2017c) Anchor-assisted and vote-based trustworthiness assurance in smart city crowdsensing. IEEE Access 4:529–541
37. Ruan N, Gao L, Zhu H, Jia W, Li X, Hu Q (2016) Toward optimal dos-resistant authentication in crowdsensing networks via evolutionary game. In: IEEE ICDCS, Nara, Japan
38. Sheng H, Zhang S, Cao X, Fang Y, Xiong Z (2017) Geometric occlusion analysis in depth estimation using integral guided filter for light-field image. IEEE Trans Image Process 26(12):5758–5771
39. Song Z, Liu CH, Wu J, Ma J, Wang W (2014) Qoi-aware multitask-oriented dynamic participant selection with budget constraints. IEEE Trans Veh Technol 63(9):4618–4632
40. Sun J, Ma H (2014) A behavior-based incentive mechanism for crowd sensing with budget constraints. In: IEEE ICC, Sydney, Australia
41. Talasila M, Curtmola R, Borcea C (2013) Improving location reliability in crowd sensed data with minimal efforts. In: IEEE WMNC, Dubai, United Arab Emirates
42. Wang B, Kong L, He L, Wu F, Yu J, Chen G (2018) I(TS, CS): detecting faulty location data in mobile crowdsensing. In: ICDCS, Vienna, Austria
43. Wang G, Wang B, Wang T, Nika A, Zheng H, Zhao BY (2016a) Defending against sybil devices in crowdsourced mapping services. In: ACM MobiSys, Singapore
44. Wang W, Gao H, Liu CH, Leung KK (2016b) Credible and energy-aware participant selection with limited task budget for mobile crowd sensing. Ad Hoc Netw 43:56–70
45. Weinsberg U, Balachandran A, Balachandran A, Balachandran A, Seshan S, Seshan S, Seshan S (2012) Care: content aware redundancy elimination for challenged networks. In: ACM HotNets workshop, Redmond, WA, USA
46. Wu J, Guo S, Huang H, Liu W, Xiang Y (2018) Information and communications technologies for sustainable development goals: State-of-the-art, needs and perspectives. IEEE Commun Surv Tutor 20(3):2389–2406
47. Wu Y, Wang Y, Hu W, Zhang X, Cao G (2016) Resource-aware photo crowdsourcing through disruption tolerant networks. In: IEEE ICDCS, Nara, Japan
48. Xiong H, Zhang D, Wang L, Chaouchi H (2015a) Emc 3: energy-efficient data transfer in mobile crowdsensing under full coverage constraint. IEEE Trans Mob Comput 14(7):1355–1368
49. Xiong H, Zhang D, Wang L, Gibson JP, Zhu J (2015b) EEMC: enabling energy-efficient mobile crowdsensing with anonymous participants. ACM TIST 6(3):39:1–39:26
50. Yürür Ö, Liu CH, Sheng Z, Leung VCM, Moreno W, Leung KK, (2016) Context-awareness for mobile sensing: a survey and future directions. IEEE Commun Surv Tutor 18(1):68–93
51. Zhang D, Huang J, Li Y, Zhang F, Xu C, He T (2014) Exploring human mobility with multisource data at extremely large metropolitan scales. In: ACM/IEEE MobiCom, Maui, HI, USA
52. Zhang S, Sheng H, Li C, Zhang J, Xiong Z (2016) Robust depth estimation for light field via spinning parallelogram operator. Comput Vis Image Underst 145:148–159
53. Zhang Y, Meratnia N, Havinga PJM (2010) Outlier detection techniques for wireless sensor networks: a survey. IEEE Commun Surv Tutor 12(2):159–170
54. Zhao C, Yang X, Yu W, Yao X, Lin J, Li X (2017) Cheating-resilient incentive scheme for mobile crowdsensing systems. In: IEEE CCNC, Las Vegas, NV, USA
55. Zhou G, Fan Y, Cui R, Bian W, Zhu X, Gai K (2018) Rocket launching: a universal and efficient framework for training well-performing light net. AAAI. Louisiana, USA, New Orleans, pp 4580–4587

Chapter 3
Compressive Sensing

Compressive Sensing (CS) is a promising theory that was proposed in 2006, and it is soon be studied and applied in electrical engineering, communication, statistics, machine learning, image processing, sensor network, and many other fields. In this chapter, we will give a brief introduction to compressive sensing and its related concepts. By reading this chapter, the readers can get: (1) the basic idea of what is compressive sensing and (2) how does compressive sensing work. The concepts and approaches mentioned in this chapter will be used throughout this book. Because, the topic of this book is the application of compressive sensing in mobile crowdsensing, and in this chapter, we just focus on *what* and *how*, while we do not dig deeply to see *why*, i.e., the strict mathematical proof that actually supports the compressive sensing theory.

3.1 Background

We live in a world surrounded by various information. In the digital era, most of the information is captured and processed by computer. From the prospect of computer, the information is a series of discrete signals. For example, a picture can be viewed as a pixel matrix, in which each pixel is a triple representing the level of *Red, Green,* and *Blue*. The temperature change in a period of time can be viewed as a time series of temperature values.

The quality of the signal is determined by its density. Typically, the denser the discrete signal is, the higher the quality is, while the size of the signal also increases. Is it possible to compress the size of the signal while still hold the quality? The answer is true, if we know the special feature of the signal. For example, consider a signal $\mathbf{y} \in \mathbb{R}^1 0$, which satisfies $\mathbf{y}[i] = \mathbf{y}[1] + (i - 1), i = 1, 2, \ldots, 10$. In this case, the signal $\mathbf{y}$ can be represented via its original 10-dimensional format, i.e., $\mathbf{y} = [y_1, y_2, \ldots, y_1 0]$, whose size is 10. With the knowledge of its special property, we can also represent it

© Springer Nature Singapore Pte Ltd. 2019
L. Kong et al., *When Compressive Sensing Meets Mobile Crowdsensing*, https://doi.org/10.1007/978-981-13-7776-1_3

as $\{y_1\}$ alone, because the other nine dimensions can be deduced from y_1. The size of the second representation is only 1, which is only 1/10 of the original representation.

Above is just an example for interpreting the possibility to compress the size while not influencing the quality of the signal. In practice, The *dimension* of the signal is much higher and the special property, if exists, is much latent. *Compressive Sensing (CS)* is the technique to capture the hidden property of the signal, and utilize the property to compress the size of the signal.

Note: the *dimension* in this chapter and the *dimension* in Chap. 7 have different meanings. In this chapter, *dimension* refer to the *length of vector*. While in Chap. 7, *dimension* refer to the information related to the data. For example, if a data is related to *time* and *location*, it is two-dimensional.

3.2 Conventional Compressive Sensing

3.2.1 Sparsity and Compressible Signals

In compressive sensing, the "special property" of the signal is called *sparsity*. In real world, the signals are typically generated by linear systems. Thus, an n-dimensional signal can be represented by a vector lives in an n-dimensional linear space $\mathbb{R}^n$. However, in most cases, it is too sumptuous to actually use an n-dimensional linear space to represent the signal. This is because in most cases, the possible values of the signal cannot fill the whole n-dimensional space. This property is vividly described as *sparsity*.

To formally describe the *sparse* property, let us first review the mathematical concept *base*.

Base: In an n-dimensional linear space, a base is a set of linearly independent vectors $\{\psi_i\}_{i=1}^n$. According to linear algebra theory, any n-dimensional vector $\mathbf{y}$ can be represented as the linear combination of these n vectors, i.e., $\mathbf{y} = x_1\psi_1 + x_2\psi_2 + \cdots + x_n\psi_n$. If we write the set of vectors as a $n \times n$ vector $\Psi = [\psi_1, \psi_2, \ldots, \psi_n]$, the above representation can be rewritten as

$$\mathbf{y} = [\psi_1, \psi_2, \ldots, \psi_n] \times \begin{bmatrix} x_1 \\ x_2 \\ \vdots \\ x_n \end{bmatrix} = \Psi\mathbf{x}, \tag{3.1}$$

where $\mathbf{x} = [x_1, x_2, \ldots, x_n]^T$ is the *coefficient vector* or *coordinate* of $\mathbf{y}$ in base Ψ.

An commonly used special case of the *base* is *orthogonal base*, in which each two vectors ψ_i and ψ_j hold the following property:

$$< \psi_i, \psi_j >= \begin{cases} 0 & i = j; \\ 1 & i \neq j, \end{cases} \tag{3.2}$$

where $< \psi_i, \psi_j >$ is the inner product of the two vectors. Orthogonal base has a convenient property that the *coordinate* $\mathbf{x}$ can be easily calculated by

$$\mathbf{x} = \Psi^T \mathbf{y}. \tag{3.3}$$

The *base* is the key to capture the *sparse* property of the signal $\mathbf{y}$. Typically, a vector is *k-sparse* if it has no more than k nonzero elements, i.e., $\mathbf{x}$ is $k - sparse$ if $\|x\|_0 \leq k$. With the help of orthogonal base, the concept can be extended so that for a signal $\mathbf{y}$, if its coordinate under a base Ψ is $k - sparse$, $\mathbf{y}$ is also $k - sparse$. This is because $\mathbf{y}$ can be easily transformed to $\mathbf{x}$ according to Eq. (3.3). Here is a naive example.

Consider a *four*-dimensional base:

$$\Psi = \begin{bmatrix} 1/2 & 1/2 & 1/2 & 1/2 \\ -1/2 & -1/2 & 1/2 & 1/2 \\ 1/2 & -1/2 & 1/2 & -1/2 \\ 1/2 & -1/2 & -1/2 & 1/2 \end{bmatrix}$$

and a *four*-dimensional signal $\mathbf{y} = [3, 1, 1, -3]^T$, the coordinate of $\mathbf{y}$ under Ψ is

$$\mathbf{x} = \Psi^T \mathbf{y} = \begin{bmatrix} 1/2 & 1/2 & 1/2 & 1/2 \\ -1/2 & -1/2 & 1/2 & 1/2 \\ 1/2 & -1/2 & 1/2 & -1/2 \\ 1/2 & -1/2 & -1/2 & 1/2 \end{bmatrix} \times \begin{bmatrix} 3 \\ 1 \\ 1 \\ -3 \end{bmatrix} = \begin{bmatrix} 0 \\ 2 \\ 4 \\ 0 \end{bmatrix},$$

which has only two nonzero elements. Thus, we call the signal $\mathbf{y}$ is 2-sparse under Ψ.

For a signal in real world, it is hard to find a base so that most elements in the coordinate is exactly zero. This is because the signals are always contaminated by noises in the ambient environment. Thus, relax the definition of *sparsity* by allowing most of the elements in the coordinate $\mathbf{x}$ close to zero, instead of exactly zero. This property is called *approximate sparsity*. Figure 3.1 shows an example of this scenario. Figure 3.1a illustrates a 100-dimensional signal, while Fig. 3.1b illustrates its coordinate under *Discrete Cosine Transform (DCT)* base. We can see from Fig. 3.1b that although most of the values in the coordinate are not exactly zero, only 5 values are significant while the others are close to zero. Thus, we call the signal in Fig. 3.1a as *(approximate) 5-sparse*.

Obviously, the data shown in Fig. 3.1 has some special properties and should be able to compress to a much smaller size. But to what extent can we compress it? The compressive sensing theory [1, 5] proves that, if an n-dimensional signal $\mathbf{y} \in \mathbb{R}^n$ is

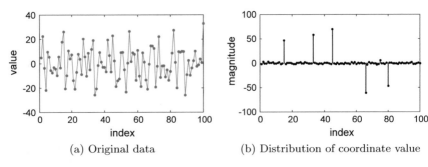

(a) Original data   (b) Distribution of coordinate value

Fig. 3.1 Example of approximate sparsity

k-sparse, we are able to accurately reconstruct it from an m-dimensional sample of it, where m satisfies:

$$m \geq k \log n. \tag{3.4}$$

According to this theorem, if n is large and k is small, the signal is compressible. For example, the 100-dimensional signal, as shown in Fig. 3.1 can be compressed to a $5 \times \log 100 = 10$ samples, which dramatically reduce the size.

3.2.2   Sampling

In compressive sensing, the procedure of compressing a compressive signal is called *sampling*. Generally speaking, "sampling" is the selection of a subset of the original dataset, and discard the other data. In Compressive sensing, the concept of sampling is extended, where the sampled data is the linear combination of the original data. Instead, here, *sampling* calculates multiple linear combination of the original signal $\mathbf{y} \in \mathbb{R}^n$, and project it into an m-dimensional vector $\mathbf{z} \in \mathbb{R}^m$. That is,

$$\mathbf{z} = \Phi \mathbf{y} = \Phi \Psi \mathbf{x}, \tag{3.5}$$

where Φ is an $m \times n$ matrix called *sampling matrix*. Typically, the *sampling matrix* Φ is deliberately designed in order to compress the signal. Thus, it is known in advance.

However, there is a special case where some data in the original signal $\mathbf{y}$ is missing. For example, consider a *four*-dimensional signal $\mathbf{y} = [y_1, y_2, y_3, y_4]^T$, if y_1 and y_3 is missing, we can represent the sampled vector $\mathbf{z}$ as follows:

$$\mathbf{z} = \Phi \mathbf{y} = \begin{bmatrix} 0 & 1 & 0 & 0 \\ 0 & 0 & 0 & 1 \end{bmatrix} \times \begin{bmatrix} y_1 \\ y_2 \\ y_3 \\ y_4 \end{bmatrix} = \begin{bmatrix} y_2 \\ y_4 \end{bmatrix}. \tag{3.6}$$

As a special case of sampling, because data missing is not controlled by human, we call it *passive sampling*. In contrast, the sampling that is deliberately designed is called *active sampling*. No matter it is *passive sampling* or *active sampling*, the *sampling matrix* Φ is always known before reconstruction. Thus, from the prospective of data reconstruction, *passive sampling* and *active sampling* are the same. In this book, we mainly utilize *passive sampling*, i.e., the data missing scenario through Chaps. 4, 5, and 6. In Chaps. 8 and 7, we also involve *active sampling*.

3.2.3 Reconstruction

Compressive sensing theory only tells us what kind of signal is compressible. However, it does not show how to reconstruct the original signal from the compressed (sampled) signal. From the discussion of Sect. 3.2.1, we know that a compressive signal y can be represented as sparse signal in specific linear space, which is represented as $y = \Psi * x$, where Ψ is a orthonormal basis and is known in advance. Thus, given a sampled signal $z = \Phi * y = \Phi * \Psi * x$, to solve the value of y is equivalent to solve the value of sparse signal x, in which most of the elements are zero. "Sparse" is the quality we know about x, and $min\|x\|_0$ depicts this quality. Thus, solve the minimization problem (3.7) can solve the value of x.

$$\begin{aligned} \text{Objective:} \ & \min \|\hat{\mathbf{x}}\|_0 \\ \text{Subject to:} \ & \mathbf{z} = \Phi\Psi\hat{\mathbf{x}}, \end{aligned} \tag{3.7}$$

where $\|\mathbf{x}\|_0$ is the l_0 norm of $\mathbf{x}$, which indicates the number of nonzero elements in $\mathbf{x}$. However, this is not applicable in practice. This is because the optimization problem (3.7) is NP-hard and cannot be solved with a reasonable time complexity.

To deal with this problem, many approaches such as l_1-minimization algorithms [2, 3, 13] and greedy algorithms [4, 6, 9, 10, 12] are proposed. The detail of these algorithms are beyond the topic of this chapter. There are many approaches to solve the compressive sensing problem. In this chapter we only briefly introduce the concept of compressive snesing and do not discuss these approaches in detail. In Chaps. 4–8, the compressive sensing is used and several solving approaches are introduced according to the applications.

3.3 Compressive Sensing for Matrix Completion

3.3.1 From Vectors to Matrices

From the above section, we know that compressive sensing is designed originally for vectors. However, in the real world, some signals are represented in matrices, e.g., images. How to apply compressive sensing on these signals stored in matrix form? A most straightforward way is to concatenate each column (or rows) of the matrix to a super long vector. For example, for an image of size 800×640, we are able to get a $800 \times 640 = 51200$ -dimensional vector by concatenating each row of the image end to end. This is what exactly many machine learning algorithms do to image data. In [14], a more concise approach is proposed, in which there is no need to transform the matrix into vector again. In the following sections (3.3.2-3.3.4), we will introduce an approach that can extend the use of compressive sensing from vectors to matrices without transforming the matrices to vectors.

3.3.2 Sparsity in Matrices

To reveal the hidden structure in matrices, we adopt *Principle Component Analysis (PCA)* on them. *PCA* is an effective nonparametric technique for simplified structure that often underlines a data set. It is a commonly used technique for analyzing high-dimensional data (or structures) [8]. Given a high-dimensional data set represented in a matrix, and its associated coordinate space, PCA can find a new coordinate space that is the best one to use for dimension reduction of the given data set. After finding this new coordinate space, we can project the high-dimensional data set onto a subset of the axes with the objective of minimizing the error. In summary, given a high-dimensional data set, we can find a small data set to approximate the original high-dimensional data set.

Any matrix X can be decomposed to three matrices according to the *Singular Value Decomposition (SVD)*:

$$X = U \Sigma V^T = \sum_{i=1}^{min(n,m)} \sigma_i u_i v_i^T , \qquad (3.8)$$

where m, n is the size of the matrix X, V^T is the transpose of V, U is a $n \times n$ unitary matrix (i.e., $U^T U = U U^T = I_{n \times n}$), V is a $m \times m$ unitary matrix, and S is a $n \times m$ diagonal matrix constraining the singular values σ_i of X. The rank of a matrix equals the number of its nonzero singular values.

According to 3.8, σ_i is a coefficient of the ith principal component, which we may explain as the energy of the ith principal component. Here, the σ_is in Σ are analogical to *coordinate* in Eq. 3.1. If most σ_is in Σ are zero, we call the matrix as *low rank* or *sparse*.

As discussed in Sect. 3.2.1, it is hard to find a matrix in real world that is *strictly low rank*. Hence, *approximate low-rank* property is proposed. To formally define the *approximate low-rank* property, without loss of generality, let us first sort the singular values σ_i in an descending order. That is,

$$\sigma_i > \sigma_{i+1}, 1 \le i \le min(m, n). \qquad (3.9)$$

If the sum of first r singular values is close to the sum of all singular values, i.e.,

$$\Sigma_{i=0}^{r}\sigma_i \geq \tau \Sigma_{i=0}^{min(m,n)}\sigma_i, \tag{3.10}$$

where τ is the percentage which is typically set to 90 or 0.95%, and $r \ll min(m, n)$, we call the matrix X is *approximate low rank*, which is analogical to *approximate sparse* in vectors.

3.3.3 Sampling in Matrices

If a matrix X is *(approximate) low rank*, we can reconstruct the original matrix from a subset of the elements in it. The sampling of a matrix X can be done with a *binary indicator matrix B*, which is a $m \times n$ matrix and is defined as

$$B[i, j] = \begin{cases} 0, & \text{if } B[i, j] \text{ is sampled out (missing),} \\ 1, & \text{otherwise.} \end{cases} \tag{3.11}$$

The sampled matrix S is defined as

$$S = B \circ X, \tag{3.12}$$

where $\circ$ is element-wise product.

3.3.4 Reconstruction in Matrices

As shown in Sect. 3.3.2, any matrix can be decomposed in such a way that it equals the multiplication of three component matrices. When the rank is fixed and set to r, to generate an estimate that approximates the original matrix, we keep the r largest components in (3.8) and drop the others. Thus,

$$\hat{X} = \sum_{i=1}^{r} \sigma_i u_i v_i = \sum_{i=1}^{r} \sigma_i A_i. \tag{3.13}$$

This $\hat{X}$ is known as the best rank-r approximation with respect to the Frobenius norm $\| \cdot \|_F$ of approximation errors, $\|X\|_F = \sqrt{\sum_{i,j} X_{i,j}^2}$ for any matrix [7]. Then, $\hat{X}$ is the solution to the following optimization problem:

$$\begin{aligned} \min \quad & \|X - \hat{X}\|_F \\ \text{s.t.} \quad & rank(\hat{X}) \leq r. \end{aligned} \tag{3.14}$$

However, it is impossible to directly apply (3.14) as we do not have the knowledge of the original matrix and the proper rank.

As a good estimate, it is reasonable to be as close as to the sampled matrix S. In addition, the estimate matrix should have a *low-rank* structure. Thus, we try to find the low-rank estimate:

$$
\begin{aligned}
&\min \ rank(\hat{X}) \\
&\text{s.t.} \quad B \circ \hat{X} = S.
\end{aligned}
\tag{3.15}
$$

It is difficult to solve this minimization problem because it is nonconvex.

To circumvent the difficulty, we make use of the SVD-like factorization, which rewrites (3.15) as follows:

$$
\hat{X} = U \Sigma V^T = L R^T,
\tag{3.16}
$$

where $L = U \Sigma^{1/2}$ and $R = V \Sigma^{1/2}$. According to the compressive sensing literature [5, 14], we can solve a simpler problem and obtain an equivalent result under a certain condition. Specifically, if the restricted isometry property [11] holds, minimizing the nuclear form can perform rank minimization exactly for a matrix of low rank. Here, if the rank of X is smaller than that of $L R^T$, then we can apply this technique. That is, we just find matrix L and R that minimize the summation of their Frobenius norms:

$$
\begin{aligned}
&\min \ \|L\|_F^2 + \|R\|_F^2 \\
&\text{s.t.} \quad B \circ (L R^T) = S.
\end{aligned}
\tag{3.17}
$$

In practice, L and R that strictly satisfy the constraint are likely to fail for two reasons. First, there are noises in the probe data, and therefore strict satisfaction may lead to the overfit problem. Second, the rank of a traffic condition matrix is only approximately low.

Thus, we use the Lagrange multiplier method to solve (3.17):

$$
min(a + \lambda b),
\tag{3.18}
$$

where

$$
\begin{aligned}
a &= \|B \circ (L R^T) - S\|_F^2, \\
b &= \|L\|_F^2 + \|R\|_F^2.
\end{aligned}
\tag{3.19}
$$

The Lagrange multiplier λ controls the trade-off between rank minimization and measurement fitness. There are many approaches to solve the compressive sensing problem. In this chapter we only briefly introduce the concept of compressive snesing and do not discuss these approaches in detail. In Chaps. 4–8, the compressive sensing is used and several solving approaches are introduced according to the applications.

3.4 Summary

In this chapter, we briefly review the principle of compressive sensing. We first introduced the concept of *sparse* of vectors, and then showed that the sparse signals are compressible and can be recovered accurately. Next, we extended the concept of *sparse* to matrices and derived the basic form of matrix completion in compressive sensing. The concepts introduced in this chapter will be used throughout the next chapters.

References

1. Baraniuk R (2007) Compressive sensing. Lecture Notes IEEE Signal Process Mag 24
2. Becker SR, Candès EJ, Grant MC (2011) Templates for convex cone problems with applications to sparse signal recovery. Math Progr Comput (MPC) 3(3):165
3. Bobin J, Becker S, Candes E (2011) A fast and accurate first-order method for sparse recovery. SIAM J Imaging Sci (SIIMS)
4. Bulmensath T, Davies M (2009) Iterative hard thresholding for compressive sensing. Appl Comput Harmonic Anal 27(3):265–274
5. Donoho DL (2006) Compressed sensing. Trans Inf Theory (TIT) 52(4):1289–1306
6. Donoho DL, Elad M, Temlyakov VN (2006) Stable recovery of sparse overcomplete representations in the presence of noise. Trans Inf Theory (TIT) 52(1):6–18
7. Lakhina A, Crovella M, Diot C (2004a) Diagnosing network-wide traffic anomalies. ACM SIGCOMM Comput Commun Rev ACM 34:219–230
8. Lakhina A, Papagiannaki K, Crovella M, Diot C, Kolaczyk ED, Taft N (2004b) Structural analysis of network traffic flows. ACM SIGMETRICS Perform Eval Rev ACM 32:61–72
9. Mallat S, Zhang Z (1993) Matching pursuit with time-frequency dictionaries. Tech. rep, Courant Institute of Mathematical Sciences New York United States
10. Needell D, Vershynin R (2009) Uniform uncertainty principle and signal recovery via regularized orthogonal matching pursuit. Found Comput Math (FoCM) 9(3):317–334
11. Recht B, Fazel M, Parrilo PA (2010) Guaranteed minimum-rank solutions of linear matrix equations via nuclear norm minimization. SIAM Rev 52(3):471–501
12. Tropp JA, Gilbert AC (2007) Signal recovery from random measurements via orthogonal matching pursuit. Trans Inf Theory (TIT) 53(12):4655–4666
13. Van Den Berg E, Friedlander MP (2008) Probing the pareto frontier for basis pursuit solutions. SIAM J Sci Comput (SISC) 31(2):890–912
14. Zhang Y, Roughan M, Willinger W, Qiu L (2009) Spatio-temporal compressive sensing and internet traffic matrices. ACM SIGCOMM Comput Commun Rev ACM 39:267–278

Chapter 4
Basic Compressive Sensing for Data Reconstruction

Compressive Sensing is a powerful tool for data reconstruction due to its ability to accurately capture the internal structure of data. Specifically, by introducing spatial–temporal and other additional information into it, the reconstruction accuracy can be further improved. In this chapter, we start with a mobile crowdsensing application—Urban Traffic Estimation. Next, we will see how the internal structure of collected data is captured by the basic compressive sensing and how the data is reconstructed. Finally, we show how to introduce spatial–temporal and other additional information into compressive sensing to further improve the accuracy of data reconstruction.

4.1 Background

Traffic social and economic activities around many cities in the congestion have a significant negative impact on world [7, 9, 11]. Road traffic monitoring aims to determine traffic conditions of different road links, which is an essential step toward active congestion control. Many tasks, such as trip planning, traffic management, road engineering, and infrastructure planning, can benefit from traffic estimation. As an example, Shanghai, the largest metropolis in China, is undergoing rapid economic growth, but meanwhile suffers constant traffic congestion. To mitigate the burden of the underlying road networks, efficient traffic management is of great importance, and metropolitan-scale traffic estimation is valuable to traffic management.

Traditional approaches for traffic monitoring rely on the use of static traffic sensors, such as inductive loop detectors and video cameras. Vehicle loop detectors and closed-circuit video cameras are usually deployed at the roadside to detect flow

This chapter is represented with permission from ©[2012] IEEE ref. Zhu, Y., Li, Z., Zhu, H., Li, M. and Zhang, Q., 2013. A compressive sensing approach to urban traffic estimation with probe vehicles. *IEEE Transactions on Mobile Computing, 12*(11), pp. 2289–2302.

© Springer Nature Singapore Pte Ltd. 2019
L. Kong et al., *When Compressive Sensing Meets Mobile Crowdsensing*, https://doi.org/10.1007/978-981-13-7776-1_4

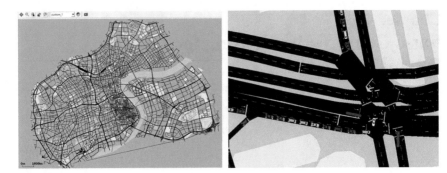

Fig. 4.1 Left: A downtown subnetwork of Shanghai, China, along with the distribution road network. Right: The real-time locations of taxis are plotted in the road network

velocity, and traffic density [3, 4, 12]. The coverage of such traditional approach is limited due to the high infrastructure deployment and maintenance cost [6]. This suggests that it is infeasible to install loop detectors and video cameras densely to cover the entire road network.

With the growing prevalence of Global Positioning System (GPS) receivers embedded in vehicles and smartphones, there have been increasing interests in using their location updates or trajectories for monitoring traffic [1, 7, 9]. We present an approach to perform metropolitan-scale traffic estimation with probe vehicles. Equipped with a GPS receiver, a probe vehicle can detect its instant location and speed. A probe vehicle periodically sends its location and speed update (or probe data report) to a monitoring center for traffic estimation. Such updates can be transmitted via the data service of a widely available cellular wireless network, such as GSM/GPRS. In Fig. 4.1, a distribution snapshot of a fleet of probe taxis over the downtown subnetwork of Shanghai is shown.

We consider the traffic condition of a road segment (or link) between two neighboring road intersections or signals in a time slot. In our approach, we use the flow speed on this link within the time slot to indicate this traffic condition, as used by previous studies [2, 12]. Since the flow speed is a random variable, we use the mean of the speed. In practice, we use the average of the speeds of probe vehicles driving on the link in the time slot to approximate the mean of the speed. This approach to traffic estimation with probe vehicles has salient advantages [7]. First, as these public vehicles traverse most of the road segments in the city, the system provides a large coverage. Second, because of the low cost of onboard GPS receivers, the overall system deployment cost is low.

Specifically, the probe data is collected via the following scheme:

- Each probe vehicle is equipped with a GPS receiver, which continuously detects instant location and speed. A probe data update includes vehicle identification, instant speed, location in longitude and latitude, and timestamp. The speed is the instantaneous speed directly provided by the GPS receiver.

- A probe data report is sent from moving vehicles to the monitoring server via a wireless data service provided by a cellular network. The typical data rate of GSM/GPRS is around 20 Kbps. The size of a probe report is relatively small, around 40 bytes. For each vehicle, probe reports are sent to the monitoring server periodically. In our approach, the reporting interval varies from 30 s to several minutes. It depends on the availability of GPRS availability. Thus, the bandwidth of GPRS is sufficient to support the delivery of probe data back to the monitoring server.

Note that, there may exist a privacy concern if each vehicle simply reports all its locations, because it may release sensitive information, such as the home location. However, it is out of the scope of this chapter to address the privacy issue. This will be discussed in Chap. 6.

It is challenging to perform traffic estimation with speed measurements from probe vehicles. Because the distribution of probe vehicles over space and time is uneven, the set of received probe data is incomplete over time and space, or contains spatiotemporal sampling vacancies. This raises a serious missing data problem for road traffic estimation. This problem has been confirmed with our analysis on the large data set of real probe data collected from a fleet of 4,000 taxis in Shanghai, China. It is important to note that probe vehicles move at their own wills. They cannot be deliberately controlled to achieve a better coverage over time and space of the set of received speed measurements. In addition, the reception of probe data is vulnerable to the influence of the urban environment. For example, when a vehicle moves through a road with surrounding tall buildings (so-called urban canyons) because of attenuation and multipath propagation of radio signals [5].

Next, we will see how compressive sensing is applied to deal with the challenge.

4.2 Problem Statement

In this section, we first define the problem, and then discuss the missing data problem.

4.2.1 Missing Data Problem in Mobile Crowdsensing

We first introduce some notations. The set of probe vehicles are denoted as N. For a probe vehicle, $v \in N$, it moves along the roads and sends its location and speed update from time to time. The update of probe data at time t is denoted by $s_v(t) :< id_v, p_v(t), q_v(t), t >$, where id_v is vehicle ID, $p_v(t)$ denotes its location (longitude and latitude), and $q_v(t)$ denotes its speed. Let T_v denote the set of timestamps at which vehicle v sends its probe data, $T_v = \{t_1^v, t_2^v, \ldots, t_k^v\}$, in which t_1^v and t_k^v are the first timestamp and the last time stamp, respectively. Thus, vehicle v has a set of probe measurements, $S_v = \{s_v(t)|t \in T_v\}$. Note that for different probe vehicles, the set of timestamps may be different.

We consider the traffic condition of a road segment between two neighboring road intersections in a given time slot. It is not straightforward to devise a single metric for quantifying the traffic condition of a given road segment at a given time. Many metrics have been proposed in the traffic engineering area for quantifying the traffic condition of a link, such as flow speed, density, length of queues [2, 7, 10]. We adopt the speed of the traffic flow on the link to indicate the traffic condition of this link, as used in previous studies [5, 12]. Since the traffic flow consists of vehicles traveling on the link, the speed of the traffic flow can be considered as the speed of a vehicle in the flow, which is a random variable. We focus on the mean of the speed to indicate the traffic condition. It is meaningful because if the flow has a higher speed, a vehicle in the flow can generally drive at a higher speed.

Thus, we formally define the traffic condition of a road segment in a given time slot as follows:

Definition 4.1 (*Traffic condition*) The traffic condition of a road segment r in a given time slot t denoted as $x_{r,t}$ is defined as the mean of the speed $\vartheta_{r,t}$ of a vehicle driving within the traffic flow on this road segment in the time slot, i.e., $x_{r,t} = E(\vartheta_{r,t})$.

In practice, we use the average of the speeds of all probe vehicles on the road segment within the time slot to approximate the mean of the flow speed. The average is computed over different probe speeds of all vehicles. In the definition of traffic condition, we have made this assumption that traffic conditions on a segment is uniform during each time slot.

It should be noted that the approach of using average speeds to indicate the traffic state of a road segment has certain limitation. By this approach, the quality of traffic states monitoring is related to the sampling process of probe vehicles. Clearly, as there are more probe data, the quality of resulting traffic states estimation is better. In our work, however, the average value of probe speeds is considered as the real state of a road segment. We do not explicitly consider the impact of the number of probe samples. We are interested in the traffic conditions of a given set of road segments at a given set of time slots T:

$$\Omega = \{r_0, r_1, r_2, \ldots, r_{n-1}\}, \tag{4.1}$$

$$T = \{t_0, t_1, t_2, \ldots, t_{n-1}\}. \tag{4.2}$$

The traffic conditions of Ω over T form a traffic condition matrix, denoted by $X_T CM$, or simply X:

$$X_{TCM} = (x_{r,t})_{m \times n}, \tag{4.3}$$

where $x_{r,t}$ is the condition or road segment r in time slot t.

It is difficult to obtain a complete traffic condition matrix as there may exist many spatiotemporal vacancies with no probe measurements. There is no guarantee that the monitoring server to receive probe measurements for each road segment within every time slot. This raises a serious missing data problem, which will be further demonstrated with empirical study with the data set of real probe data in Sect. 4.2.2.

In fact, we are given a measurement matrix $M = [m_{r,t}]_{m \times n}$:

$$M_{TCM} = X_{TCM} \circ B, \tag{4.4}$$

where $\circ$ is dot product operator and B is an indicator matrix of size $m \times n$, and is defined as follows:

$$B[i, j] = \begin{cases} 0, & \text{if no probe data for } r \text{ in slot } t, \\ 1, & \text{otherwise.} \end{cases} \tag{4.5}$$

The goal is to obtain an estimate $\hat{X}$ for X when given M, with the objective of minimizing the normalized mean absolute error of the estimate, which is defined as follows:

Definition 4.2 (*Normalized mean absolute error*) The normalized mean absolute error of an estimate $\hat{X}$ for X is

$$\psi = \sum_{r,t:m_{r,t}=0} |x_{r,t} - \hat{x}_{r,t}| / \sum_{r,t:m_{r,t}=0} |x_{r,t}|. \tag{4.6}$$

Then, we formally define the problem as follows:

Definition 4.3 (*Traffic estimation problem*) Given the set of probe measurements from probe vehicles, the traffic estimation problem is first to obtain the measurement matrix M, and then to find an estimate $\hat{X}$ for the real traffic condition matrix X, with the objective of minimizing the normalized mean absolute error of the estimate $\hat{X}$.

4.2.2 Sparse and Uneven Data Distribution

We show the sparse and uneven distribution of the set of received probe measurements from probe vehicles, which raises the serious missing data problem.

We first define a metric of integrity as follows:

Definition 4.4 Let B be the indicator matrix for matrix M. The integrity of M, denoted by ϖ, is defined as the fraction of nonzero elements:

$$\varpi(M) = \frac{sum(B)}{size(B)}. \tag{4.7}$$

We analyze the impact of the number of probe vehicles on the integrity of the measurement matrix by extracting the probe data of a subset of probe vehicles from the complete set of probe data. We analyze the sets of probe data of 500, 1,000,

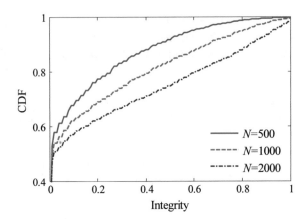

Fig. 4.2 CDF of integrity of roads

Table 4.1 Integrity summery (February 18, 2007)

Time gran. (min)	$N = 500$ (%)	$N = 1,000$ (%)	$N = 2,000$ (%)
15	12.22	18.28	24.80
30	18.57	25.18	31.61
60	25.53	31.98	37.64

and 2,000 taxis over a duration of 24 h on February 18, 2007, respectively. All the taxis were running in the inner region of Shanghai, in which there are 5,812 road segments. By default, we set the time granularity (i.e., the length of time slot) to 15 min in this empirical study.

First, we study the integrity for a given road segment, by which we can learn the missing data issue over time. Figure 4.2 shows the empirical cumulative distribution functions (CDFs) of integrity of all roads under different numbers of vehicles, i.e., 500, 1,000, and 2,000. We can see that when there are 500 probe vehicles, nearly 95% of roads have an integrity of less than 60%. This means that these roads have no probe measurements for more than 40% of time. Generally, when we deploy more probe vehicles, the integrity can be improved. However, even when 2,000 probe vehicles are employed, there are still nearly 80% of roads whose integrity is less than 60%. More importantly, we find that nearly 50% of road segments have an integrity close to zero. This indicates that no vehicles have traveled through these road segments within some single slots.

Next, we consider the integrity at a given time snapshot. In this way, we can learn the missing data issue over space. In Fig. 4.3, we plot the CDFs of integrity of all time slots under different numbers of probe vehicles, i.e., 500, 1,000, and 2,000. We can see that when there are 500 probe vehicles, nearly 100% of time slots have an integrity of less than 18%. This indicates that almost for all slots, more than 82% of road segments have no probe measurements.

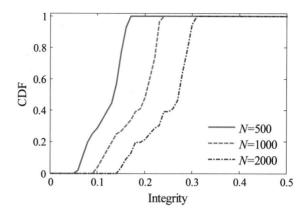

Fig. 4.3 CDF of integrity of time slots

Finally, we study the integrity of measurement matrices for different time granularities. Table 4.1 shows the integrities under different time granularities when there are 500, 1,000, and 2,000 probe vehicles. We can find that even when there are 2,000 probe vehicles, the integrity is as low as 24.8% when the time granularity is 15 min and 37.64% when the time granularity is 60 min.

In summary, we find that the missing data problem is serious. The possible solution to improve the integrity is to deploy more probe vehicles. However, this may increase cost, and be impractical in some situations, for example, there is no way to employ more probe vehicles.

4.3 Basic Compressive Sensing Algorithm

The goal is to compute an estimate of the traffic condition matrix for the real traffic condition matrix with the objective of minimizing the estimate error. A compressive sensing-based algorithm is used to effectively exploit the hidden structures.

4.3.1 Revealing Hidden Structure

The traffic conditions of different road segments over different times are not independent. There exist structures. We reveal such hidden structures by using principal component analysis. We use the same data set of probe data collected from the fleet of taxis in Shanghai, China, as introduced previously.

As described in Sect. 3.3.2, the *low-rank* property can be revealed by its singular values. In Fig. 4.4, we present the magnitude (ratio to the maximum) of singular values. This figure suggests that most of the energy is contributed by the first few principal components. The existence of the sharp knee is a result of some com-

Fig. 4.4 Magnitude of
singular values (with log
scale x-axis)

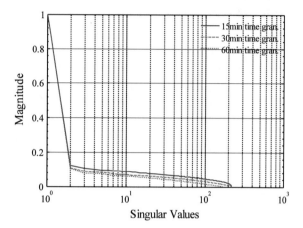

mon structures among different interested road segments, which will lead the traffic
condition matrix to a low rank.

In summary, our empirical study using the principal component analysis demonstrates that there are hidden structures with traffic condition matrices. This lays the
foundation for our compressive sensing-based algorithm for estimating missing traffic conditions.

4.3.2 Missing Data Reconstruction

We have revealed that there exist hidden structures in traffic condition matrices. Thus,
compressive sensing can be used for reconstruction. As shown in Sect. 3.3.4, perform
compressive sensing reconstruction is equivalent to solve the following optimization
problem:

$$\min(a + \lambda b), \tag{4.8}$$

where

$$
\begin{aligned}
a &= \| B \circ (L R^T) - M \|_F^2, \\
b &= \| L \|_F^2 + \| R \|_F^2.
\end{aligned}
\tag{4.9}
$$

Many ways can solve the above optimization problem. We propose an algorithm
that is similar to the one in [13]. We show the detail pseudocode in Algorithm 4.1.
The algorithm starts with a random initialization to matrix L. It first fixes matrix L
and then computes matrix R. Next, R is fixed and L is computed. This process repeats
for a fixed number of iterations. In implementation, we perform experiments to find
a good setting of the number of iterations. In each iteration, we have to compute
either L or R to minimize the objective (4.8). We find that reaching the objective is
equivalent to making both x and y equal to zero simultaneously. Thus, we have the

---

Algorithm 4.1: Basic compressive sensing for matrix estimation.

Input : Measurement Matrix $M_{m \times n}$; Indicator Matrix $B_{m \times n}$; Rank Bound r; Trade-off
  Coefficient λ; Iteration Times t
Output: Estimate Matrix $\hat{X}_{m \times n}$
1 $L \leftarrow$ random_matrix(m, r);
2 **for** $k \leftarrow 1$ *to* t **do**
3 $\quad R \leftarrow$ inverse$([L; \sqrt{\lambda}I], [M; 0])$;
4 $\quad L \leftarrow$ inverse$([R^T; \sqrt{\lambda}I], [M^T; 0])$;
5 $\quad v \leftarrow \|B. \times (LR^T) - M\|_F^2 + \lambda(\|L\|_F^2 + \|R^T\|_F^2)$;
6 $\quad$ **if** $v < \hat{v}$ **then**
7 $\quad\quad \hat{L} \leftarrow L; \hat{R} \leftarrow R; \hat{v} \leftarrow v$;

8 $\hat{X} \leftarrow \hat{L} \times \hat{R}^T$;
9 **return** $\hat{X}$;

---

following when L is given:

$$\begin{bmatrix} B \circ (LR^T) \\ R \end{bmatrix} = \begin{bmatrix} M \\ 0 \end{bmatrix}. \tag{4.10}$$

This is a contradictory equation, because the number of constraints is larger than that of unknown variables. By computing the best approximate solution to this contradictory equation with least squares, we can compute the best matrix R for satisfying 4.8.

We analyze the complexity of the algorithm as follows: the key operation of Algorithm 4.1 is the procedure for computing an inverse matrix, which gives the best approximate solution to the contradictory equation. The procedure is essentially completed by a matrix multiplication. Therefore, its complexity is $O(rmn)$, where r, m, n denote the column number of L, the row number of X, and the column number of X, respectively. The algorithm repeats the procedure for t times. Therefore, the total complexity of the algorithm is $O(rmnt)$. Note that t is a design parameter of Algorithm 4.1. Through experiments, we find that the setting of $t = 100$ makes the algorithm to converge to a steady output when the matrix size is of hundreds by hundreds.

4.3.3 Design Optimizations

Two important parameters must be determined in Algorithm 4.1, i.e., rank bound r and trade-off coefficient λ. The two parameters greatly influence the final estimate quality. According to the principle of compressive sensing, the rank of the approximated matrix should be minimized. In Algorithm 4.1, r is the number of columns in matrix L and R, which is smaller than m and n. Thus, we have

---

Algorithm 4.2: Finding optimal parameters.

Input : Lower Bound and Upper Bound of r: $\ell_r, \mathcal{U}_r$; Lower Bound and Upper Bound of λ:
 $\ell_\lambda, \mathcal{U}_\lambda$; Measurement Matrix B
Output: Optimal r and λ

1 $\mathcal{N}(population) \leftarrow$ initialize with random numbers of uniformly distributed within $[\ell_r, \mathcal{U}_r]$
   and $[\ell_\lambda, \mathcal{U}_\lambda]$;
2 **while** ***not*** *stall(fitness)* **do**
3 | $\mathcal{H} \leftarrow$ select($\mathcal{N}$);
4 | $\mathcal{C} \leftarrow$ crossover($\mathcal{N}$);
5 | $\mathcal{M} \leftarrow$ mutate($\mathcal{N}$);
6 | $\mathcal{N} \leftarrow [\mathcal{H}, \mathcal{C}, \mathcal{M}]$;
7 $[r, \lambda] \leftarrow$ decode(the best individual in $\mathcal{N}$);

$$rank(\hat{X}) \leq \min(rank(L), rank(R)) = r. \tag{4.11}$$

Thus, r is an upper bound of $rank(\hat{X})$, and impacts the algorithm performance.

We should determine the optimal parameters in order for Algorithm 4.1 to obtain the best performance in terms of estimate error. However, it is not trivial to determine the optimal parameters. The quality of estimation is a function of the two parameters, denoted by $\ell = f(r, \lambda)$, Then, to obtain the optimal parameters, the objective is as follows:

$$\max \ell = \max f(r, \lambda). \tag{4.12}$$

We use estimate error to indicate the quality of estimation. The definition of estimate error will be given in the next section. The key issue is that function $f(\cdot)$ characterizing the relationship between error and the parameters is invisible.

We propose a genetic algorithm for deriving the optimal parameters of rank bound and trade-off coefficient. The strength of this algorithm is that the analytical form of the objective is not needed. In this algorithm, estimate errors are used as fitness. We encode the two parameters as a vector that contains two real numbers. The pseudocode is shown in Algorithm 4.2.

We explain the main steps of the algorithm in the following:

1. *Initialization.* We randomly initialize the population representing the two parameters. The size of population is a design parameter of this algorithm.
2. *Selection.* Each individual is evaluated against fitness. The fitness function is the estimate error, which can be evaluated by invoking Algorithm 4.2 with the parameters encoded by each individual. Then, the best individuals are selected to breed the next generation.
3. *Reproduction.* Besides the group of individuals selected in the selection process, the next generation also includes two other groups. By employing the roulette model, one group of offsprings is produced by taking the crossover of any two individuals, and the other group of offsprings are produced by the mutation operation. Specifically, we assign a random value to one of the parameters within its domain to achieve the mutation.

4. *Termination.* The algorithm can terminate after a fixed number of integrations or after a threshold on fitness improvement is met. We adopt a fixed number of iterations as the termination criterion.

There are several design parameters with Algorithm 4.2, including bounds of rank bound and trade-off coefficient, size of population, and number of iterations. The lower bound of rank bound r can be set to 1 because it is positive, and its upper bound is given by (4.11). It is not easier to determine the bounds of trade-off coefficient, we determine the bounds by experiments. The size of population and the number of iterations are also determined by experiments.

The time complexity of Algorithm 4.2 can be high because each time an individual evaluated its fitness, Algorithm 4.1 should be invoked to get the estimate error. Fortunately, however, Algorithm 4.2 is only executed once for a given set of road segments. With experiments, we find that for a given set of road segments, the two parameters obtained by Algorithm 4.2 are stable over different times.

4.4 Experiments and Analysis

We have performed extensive experiments for evaluating the performance of the proposed algorithm for traffic estimation. In the following, we first present the methodology and the experimental setup. The compared algorithms are then introduced. Finally, performance results are presented and discussed.

4.4.1 Methodology and Experimental Setup

Experiments are conducted with two data sets of probe data. One data set is from the fleet of 4,000 taxis in Shanghai, as introduced before, and the other data set of probe data is from a fleet of 8,000 taxis in Shenzhen, China. Both data sets of probe data span a duration of 1 week. Three-time granularities, i.e., 15, 30, and 60 min, are used.

We choose a subnetwork of 221 road segments in Shanghai, and a subnetwork of 198 road segments in Shenzhen for experiments. Both subnetworks are from a region close to city centers. In comparison, Shanghai is more dense than Shenzhen, in terms of distribution of probe vehicles. The major reason for choosing downtown regions is that we need to know the original traffic condition matrix as the ground truth. In reality, it is very difficult to find a fully integral matrix without vacancies. For this reason, it is better to find a matrix that is as integral as possible. When performing experiments, we randomly discard some elements to form measurement matrices. Then, these estimates are compared with the original matrices and estimate errors can be computed because the original matrices have only a few unavailable elements.

Note that the calculation of estimate error does not include those elements that are unavailable in the original matrices.

4.4.2 Compared Algorithms

We compare our algorithm with three other algorithms.

4.4.2.1 Naive KNN

K-Nearest Neighbors is a simple algorithm, but it is often used to solve many machine learning problems including recovery of missing values. The naive KNN interpolates missing values by taking the average of its nearest K neighbors in the measurement matrix.

4.4.2.2 Correlation-Based KNN

The correlation-based KNN is more sophisticated compared to the naive one. It calculates the average by using the K neighbors from its immediate rows or columns. In the following, we use rows as an example. The key idea is that for average computation, the candidate value is weighed by the coefficient of the current row and the candidate row:

$$w_{i,k} = |C_{i,k}| / \sum_{t=i\pm1, i\pm2} |C_{i,k}|. \tag{4.13}$$

Thus, the estimate for a missing element is computed by

$$x_{i,j} = \sum_{k=i\pm1, i\pm2} x_{k,j} w_{i,k}, \tag{4.14}$$

where $C_{i,k}$ is the correlation coefficient of row i and k.

4.4.2.3 Multichannel Singular Spectrum Analysis

MSSA is often used to solve missing data problems, for example, geographic data and meteorological data. It is a data adaptive and nonparametric method based on the embedded lag-covariance matrix. We adopt an iterative procedure proposed in [14] that utilizes the internal periodicity of traffic conditions.

4.4.3 Results

4.4.3.1 Impact of Integrity

The four algorithms are compared in terms of estimate error when the integrity of
the traffic matrix is varied. In Naive KNN, K is set to 4. In the correlative KNN, K
is also set to 4. And in MSSA, the parameter M is set to 24 as suggested by Zhu et
al. [14]. According to the result of Algorithm 4.2, we set r and λ in Algorithm 4.1
to 2 and 100, respectively.

In Fig. 4.5, the performance of the four algorithms in terms of estimate error with
Shanghai data set is shown. Three-time granularities are used, i.e., 15, 30, and 60
min. We can see that our algorithm performs the best among all the algorithms under
every time granularity. Naive KNN performs the worst. Correlation-based KNN and
MSSA are better than naive KNN, but worse than our algorithm. The two algorithms, correlation-based KNN and MSSA, produce an almost similar performance
of estimate error.

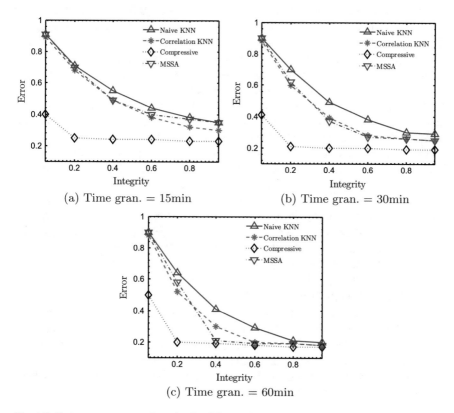

Fig. 4.5 Estimate error versus integrity for different time granularities (with Shanghai Data Set, #
of road segments = 221, # of probe vehicles = 2,000, time length = one week)

We can also find that when the integrity of the traffic condition matrix decreases, our algorithm steadily produces low estimate errors. That is, the performance of our algorithm is relatively insensitive to the integrity of measurement matrices. Even when the integrity is as low as 20%, the estimate error is no more than 20% when the time granularity is 60 min. This shows that our algorithm can reliably recover the missing elements when just a few elements are available. In contrast, the rest algorithms including naive KNN, correlation-based KNN, and MSSA have worse performance when the integrity becomes poorer. The reason is that our compressive sensing-based algorithm can effectively capture the internal structures that exist in the data set even just a few data points are used, while the rest algorithms fail to achieve this.

From Fig. 4.5, we can also see that the estimate error becomes higher when the time granularity is smaller for all algorithms. It is mainly due to the fact that the hidden structure feature of the traffic condition matrix becomes weaker because of average speeds in the traffic condition matrix would experience more variations over time when the time window is smaller. Our approach accordingly becomes less capable to accurately recover missing values.

We observe that as the integrity increases from 0.05 to 0.95, the estimate error achieved by our compressive-based algorithm first quickly decreases before the integrity is 40% and then further becomes smaller but the speed of decrease is very small. This shows that the compressive sensing-based algorithm has the strength that using only a small subset of the complete set of traffic conditions it is able to capture the majority information of the complete data set.

However, there consistently remains an estimate error of around 20% even if the integrity is as high as 95%. There are two main reasons. First, in the real world, a traffic condition may contain unpredictable randomness, which is unable to be captured by other traffic conditions. Second, there is a limitation with our compressive-based approach, which mainly focuses on linear structures of a traffic condition matrix while a real traffic condition matrix has other kinds of structures.

In Fig. 4.6, the performance of the algorithms with Shenzhen data set is shown. Since MSSA runs very slowly, we do not include MSSA in this experiment. We can find similar results as in Fig. 4.5. By comparing the impact of the two data sets, we find that the estimate error with Shenzhen data set in the same configuration is higher than that of Shanghai. This is because the probe taxies in Shanghai is more densely distributed over the subnetwork under investigation.

We further show the distribution of individual errors in Figs. 4.7 and 4.8. Since absolute errors may differ dramatically, we instead study relative errors. A relative error of an estimated element is defined as $|\hat{x}_{i,j} - x_{i,j}|/x_{i,j}$. The experiments are conducted with integrity of 20%. In Fig. 4.7, we can find that 80% of estimated elements have a relative error of smaller than 0.25 when the time granularity is 60 min. Even when the time granularity is 15 min, the relative error for nearly 80% of estimated elements is less than 0.38.

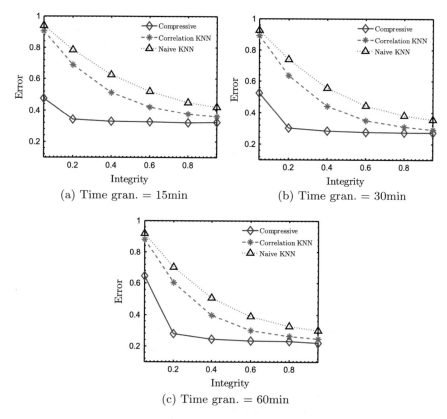

(a) Time gran. = 15min

(b) Time gran. = 30min

(c) Time gran. = 60min

Fig. 4.6 Estimate error versus integrity for different time granularities (with Shanghai Data Set, # of road segments = 221, # of probe vehicles = 2,000, time length = one week)

Fig. 4.7 CDFs of relative errors with different time granularities (Integrity = 20%, Shanghai data set)

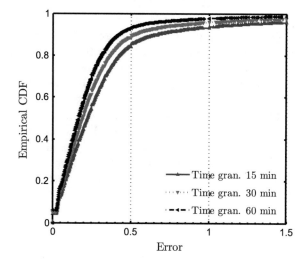

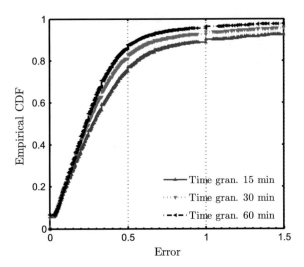

Fig. 4.8 CDFs of relative errors with different time granularities (Integrity = 20%, Shenzhen data set)

4.4.3.2 Impact of Rank Bound and Trade-off Coefficient

As mentioned before, Algorithm 4.1 has two important parameters, i.e., rank bound and trade-off coefficient. The parameters impact the performance of the algorithm. We have proposed the genetic-based algorithm for finding the optimal parameters. In the following, we conduct experiments to study the impact of these parameters and show that it is important to design the algorithm for finding the optimal parameters. The experiments are conducted with Shanghai data set.

First, we study the impact of rank bound r. In Fig. 4.9, the error rates against different rank bounds are plotted. In this experiment, the time granularity is 30 min and λ is set to one. We find that the estimate error is lowest when the rank bound is two. The main reason is that when the rank of $\hat{X}$ is low, the estimate matrix embodies the major trend of variation of the original matrix. When the rank of $\hat{X}$ grows, the estimate matrix tries to describe more information but is often misled by measurement errors. This increases the estimate error.

We also study the impact of trade-off coefficient λ. For ease of studying its impact, we set rank bound r to 32. In Fig. 4.10, estimate errors against different trade-off coefficients are shown. We find that the estimate error changes significantly when the trade-off coefficient changes from 0.001 to 2, 000. The optimal coefficient is around 100 when the rank bound is 32. A larger λ puts more weight to rank minimization and a smaller λ more emphasizes measurement fitness. A good trade-off coefficient should strike a balance between rank minimization and measurement fitness.

Fig. 4.9 Estimate error
against rank bound r ($\lambda = 1$,
granularity = 30 min,
Shanghai data set)

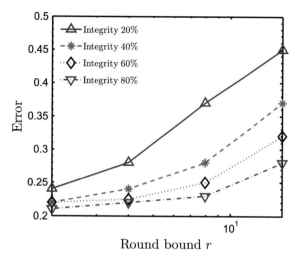

Fig. 4.10 Estimate error
against trade-off coefficient
λ ($r = 32$, granularity = 30
min, Shanghai data set)

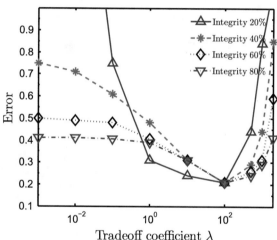

4.4.3.3 Impact of Traffic Matrix Selection

We next explore the impact of traffic matrix formation on the estimation quality of a
given road segment. According to the definition of traffic condition matrix, a column
in a traffic matrix represents a road segment, and a row represents a time instance. For
traffic estimation, we can form different traffic matrices by selecting different road
segments. For this study, we focus on the estimation quality of a given road segment,
denoted as r_0, when we select different sets of road segments for constructing traffic
matrices.

We construct five different traffic matrices by selecting five sets of road segments
as follows: note that each set contains r_0. Set 1 has six other road segments all

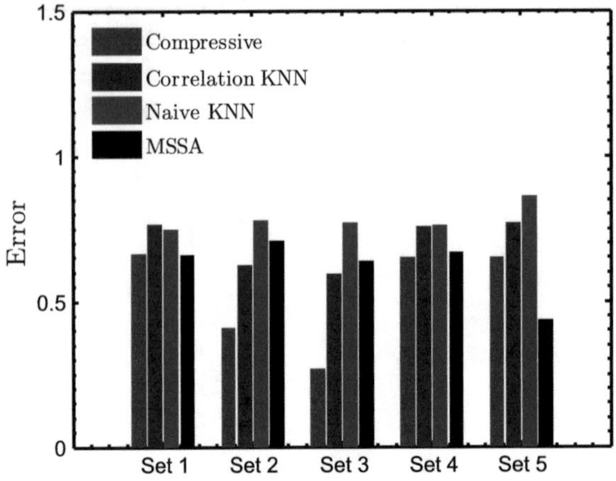

Fig. 4.11 Estimate errors
achieved by different
matrices formed by different
road segments (time
granularity = 30 min,
integrity = 20%, Shanghai
data set)

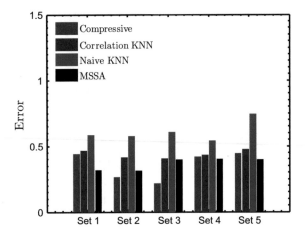

Fig. 4.12 Estimate errors
achieved by different
matrices formed by different
road segments (time
granularity = 30 min,
integrity = 40%, Shanghai
data set)

directly connected with r_0. Set 2 consists of 18 road segments within two blocks
but excluding those directly connecting ones. Set 3 has 45 randomly selected road
segments from the rest set of road segments excluding Set 2 and Set 3. Set 4 contains
six road segments randomly selected from Set 2. Set 5 contains six road segments
randomly selected from Set 3.

Estimate errors achieved by different algorithms with the five different traffic
matrices with 20% integrity and 40% integrity are shown in Figs. 4.11 and 4.12,
respectively. We find that when the number of road segments in the matrix is small
and fixed, there is no significant difference when we use different road segments to
construct the traffic matrix. In addition, the performance gain of our algorithm over
other algorithms are not significant.

However, as the number of road segments increases, for example, from Set 1 to
Set 2 and Set 3, the performance advantage of our algorithm becomes more evident.
In the case of Set 3, which contains 45 road segments, the estimate error achieved by

our algorithm is significantly better than the other competing algorithms. Thus, our proposed algorithm prefers to constructing larger matrices with more road segments, which is beneficial to making use of more evident hidden structures within traffic condition matrices.

4.5 Improvements of Compressive Sensing

So far, we have seen the original form of compressive sensing in data reconstruction, which can be summarized as the following optimization problem:

$$\min \|B \circ (LR^T) - M\|_F^2 + \lambda(\|L\|_F^2 + \|R\|_F^2). \tag{4.15}$$

This form is quite simple. In practice, other than low-rank property, the data usually has additional information. What are the types of additional information? How much does the additional information contribute? How the exploit and take advantage of the these additional information? That depends on the type of the collected data.

Two most frequently used types of additional information are *temporal stability* and *spatial stability* properties.

The temporal stability property indicates that the value is not likely to change drastically between adjacent timeslots (in other words, in a short time). This is true for most sensory data. The temporal stability property can be captured via an additional temporal term in Eq. 4.15:

$$\|LR^T\mathbb{T}\|_F^2, \tag{4.16}$$

where $\mathbb{T}$ is the temporal constraint matrix, which is defined as follows:

$$\mathbb{T} = \begin{bmatrix} 1 & -1 & 0 & \dots & 0 \\ 0 & 1 & -1 & \ddots & \vdots \\ 0 & 0 & 1 & \ddots & 0 \\ \vdots & \vdots & \ddots & \ddots & -1 \\ 0 & 0 & \dots & 0 & 1 \end{bmatrix}_{t \times t}. \tag{4.17}$$

Equation 4.16 represents for the magnitude of differences of sensory data between adjacent timeslots. If the data is temporally stable, the value of this term should be small.

The spatial stability property indicates that the data collected from locations that are spatially close enough should not have huge differences. This is true in most cases.

There are many ways to utilize spatial stability property. Here is an example method, which works only the users do not move during the data collection period. In this method, first, you need to decide how "close" the two locations should be to be defined as "neighbors". If two locations are "neighbors", the data collected from them should not be much different. The "neighbors" information can be depicted by a matrix H, which is defined as follows:

$$H(i, j) = \begin{cases} 1, & \text{if user } i \text{ and user } j \text{ are neighbors,} \\ 0, & \text{otherwise.} \end{cases} \tag{4.18}$$

Then, we define another matrix D, which is an $n \times n$ diagonal matrix defined with central diagonal given by $diag(d_1, d_2, \ldots, d_n)$, and the others given by 0. In D, $d_i = -\sum H_{(i)}$. The spatial constraint matrix $\mathbb{H}$ is defined as a row-normalized H^*, where $H^* = H + D$. For example, if we have an H:

$$H = \begin{bmatrix} 0 & 1 & 0 & 1 \\ 1 & 0 & 1 & 1 \\ 0 & 1 & 0 & 0 \\ 1 & 1 & 0 & 0 \end{bmatrix}, \tag{4.19}$$

then,

$$H^* = H + D = \begin{bmatrix} -2 & 1 & 0 & 1 \\ 1 & -3 & 1 & 1 \\ 0 & 1 & -1 & 0 \\ 1 & 1 & 0 & -2 \end{bmatrix}, \tag{4.20}$$

thus, the corresponding spatial constraint matrix is

$$\mathbb{H} = \begin{bmatrix} 1 & -1/2 & 0 & -1/2 \\ -1/3 & 1 & -1/3 & -1/3 \\ 0 & -1 & 1 & 0 \\ -1/2 & -1/2 & 0 & 1 \end{bmatrix}. \tag{4.21}$$

The spatial stability property is captured by $\mathbb{H}$. Computing the result of $\|\mathbb{H} L R^T\|_F^2$ is to get the matrix of differences between the elements and the average value of their "neighbors".

After adding temporal stability and spatial stability properties, the form of compressive sensing problem becomes:

$$\min \|B \circ (L R^T) - M\|_F^2 + \lambda(\|L\|_F^2 + \|R\|_F^2) + \|L R^T \mathbb{T}\|_F^2 + \|\mathbb{H} L R^T\|_F^2. \tag{4.22}$$

This form of compressive sensing is called *ESTI-CS* (Environmental Spatiotemporal Improved Compressive Sensing) [8]. Depending on the type of data, variables of additional information can be added. For example, in Sect. (5.3.3), we introduce the changing rate (velocity) into compressive sensing to further increase the data reconstruction accuracy.

4.6   Summary

In this chapter, starting from an example, we saw how to use compressive sensing as a powerful tool for data reconstruction in mobile crowdsensing. With principal component analysis, we have analyzed a large data set of real probe data collected from a fleet of 4,000 taxis in Shanghai, China, and discover that road traffic condition matrices often embody hidden structures or redundancy. Inspired by this observation, we have designed the basic compressive sensing algorithm, which effectively exploits the internal structures of traffic condition matrices. Experiments with the large data set of probe data have verified that the algorithm significantly outperforms other competing algorithms, including two variations of KNN and MSSA. At last, we briefly introduce how to further improve the accuracy of compressive sensing by utilizing additional information contained by the data.

References

1. Bar-Gera H (2007) Evaluation of a cellular phone-based system for measurements of traffic speeds and travel times: a case study from israel. Transp Res Part C Emerg Technol 15(6):380–391
2. Bejan AI, Gibbens RJ (2011) Evaluation of velocity fields via sparse bus probe data in urban areas. In: Intelligent transportation systems (ITSC). IEEE, pp 746–753
3. Bramberger M, Brunner J, Rinner B, Schwabach H (2004) Real-time video analysis on an embedded smart camera for traffic surveillance. In: Real-time and embedded technology and applications symposium (RTAS). IEEE, pp 174–181
4. Coifman B (2002) Estimating travel times and vehicle trajectories on freeways using dual loop detectors. Transp Res Part A Policy Pract 36(4):351–364
5. Gao B, Coifman B (2006) Vehicle identification and GPS error detection from a LIDAR equipped probe vehicle. In: International conference on intelligent transportation systems (ITSC), vol 1 (Citeseer)
6. Herrera JC, Bayen AM (2007) Traffic flow reconstruction using mobile sensors and loop detector data
7. Herring R, Hofleitner A, Abbeel P, Bayen A (2010) Estimating arterial traffic conditions using sparse probe data. In: International conference on intelligent transportation systems (ITSC). IEEE, pp 929–936
8. Kong L, Xia M, Liu XY, Wu MY, Liu X (2013) Data loss and reconstruction in sensor networks. In: International conference on computer communications (INFOCOM). IEEE, pp 1654–1662
9. Lu S, Knoop VL, Keyvan-Ekbatani M (2018) Using taxi GPS data for macroscopic traffic monitoring in large scale urban networks: calibration and MFD derivation. Transp Res Procedia 34:243–250
10. Viti F, Van Zuylen H (2006) Consistency of random queuing models at signalized intersections. In: 85th annual meeting of the transportation research board

11. Wang Y, Ding Y, Wu Q, Wei Y, Qin B, Wang H (2018) Privacy-preserving cloud-based road condition monitoring with source authentication in vanets. IEEE Trans Inf Forensics Secur
12. Work DB, Blandin S, Tossavainen OP, Piccoli B, Bayen AM (2010) A traffic model for velocity data assimilation. Appl Math Res Express 1:1–35
13. Zhang Y, Roughan M, Willinger W, Qiu L (2009) Spatio-temporal compressive sensing and internet traffic matrices. ACM SIGCOMM Comput Commun Rev 39:267–278 (ACM)
14. Zhu H, Zhu Y, Li M, Ni LM (2009) Seer: metropolitan-scale traffic perception based on lossy sensory data. In: Conference on computer communications (INFOCOM). IEEE, pp 217–225

Chapter 5
Iterative Compressive Sensing for Fault Detection

In Chap. 4, we focused on the missing data problem in mobile crowdsensing, and saw how the basic compressive sensing improves the reconstruction accuracy. In this chapter, we will discuss another issue in mobile crowdsensing—faulty data. Generally speaking, faulty data can be easily detected via traditional approaches like time series. However, due to the openness of mobile crowdsensing applications, both faulty data and missing values prevail in it. In this case, the problem becomes intractable because traditional outlier detection approaches like time series typically do not take missing value into consideration, and hence they lose effectiveness when missing values increase. In this chapter, we take a specific type of data—location data as an example, and show how compressive sensing is modified and helps solving the problem.

5.1 Background

By the definition of mobile crowdsensing, the devices for information collecting is owned by users instead of settled by authority. It has the following implications:

- The quality of the collected data is closely related to the quality of the devices and how the users operate their devices, which cannot be controlled by the application provider and cannot be guaranteed.
- Anyone with a mobile device can participant the sensing tasks, and contribute his data. This exposes the MCS system to malicious and erroneous users, who are likely to upload faulty or biased data [13].

This chapter is represented with permission from ©[2018] IEEE ref. Wang, B., Kong, L., He, L., Wu, F., Yu, J. and Chen, G., 2018, July. I (TS, CS): Detecting faulty location data in mobile crowdsensing. In *2018 IEEE 38th International Conference on Distributed Computing Systems (ICDCS)* (pp. 808–817).

© Springer Nature Singapore Pte Ltd. 2019
L. Kong et al., *When Compressive Sensing Meets Mobile Crowdsensing*, https://doi.org/10.1007/978-981-13-7776-1_5

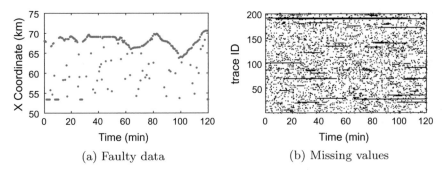

Fig. 5.1 Example of faulty data and missing values

We may name this property of mobile crowdsensing as *openness*. Due to the openness property, a large amount of faulty data and missing values may exist in the data collected by mobile crowdsensing.

Next, let us have a look at a special and important data type: location data.

Figure 5.1 illustrates an example of faulty data and missing values in MCS location data obtained from a real trace that records the trajectories of over 2,000 taxies in the urban area of Shanghai. Figure 5.1a illustrates a 2-h trace of a taxi. The location is collected every 30 s. We can easily infer the route of the taxi from the trace, and the points that deviates from the route are faulty data. By statistics, 28% of the trace are faulty. Figure 5.1b illustrates missing values of the data set that consists of traces of 200 taxies in 2 h. The black point indicates the corresponding data is missing. By statistics, 11% of the total data are missing. Such faulty data and missing values can severely deteriorate the performance of MCS applications, thus it is crucial to filter out faulty data in the presence of missing values.

Much effort has been denoted to truth discovery and data integrity in MCS [5, 8, 10–12, 17, 19], with twofold core idea: taking advantages of user reputation and designing incentive mechanism. These approaches assume that multiple observations for the same object are uploaded by different participants at the same time. However, location data is unique among participants, thus multiple observations may not be available. As a result, reputation-based error monitoring approaches are not applicable. Incentive mechanisms focus on ensuring the user to report correct data. However, they cannot avoid unintentional false data caused by sensor errors or transmission errors. Traditional outlier detection techniques [6] are alternatives for faulty data detection. However, these techniques do not take missing values into consideration.

On the other hand, as we have learned, compressive sensing is an effective way to reconstruct incomplete data set. However, it does not work well when faulty data exists. Efforts have been denoted to compensate this. Reference [4] attempts to decompose a noisy and not low-rank matrix into several components including a low-rank and an error component. However, the framework cannot automatically detect faulty data.

To address these, we focus on the problem of faulty location data detection in the presence of missing values. The major challenges are twofold: (i) existing solutions require multiple observations, which are not available for location data because it is user-specific; (ii) false positive and false negative are coupled and the trade-off between them limits the performance of faulty data detection.

In this chapter, we propose an Iterative Time-Series and Compressive Sensing $I(TS,CS)$ framework to detect and correct faulty data in MCS, which does not demand multiple observations. Specifically, $I(TS,CS)$ (i) detects and filters the faulty data via TS-based approaches, producing extremely low false negative rate (i.e., high recall), (ii) reconstructs the data set by CS to fill the missing values, and (iii) repeats the process until convergence. The iterative execution of TS and CS facilitates to bypass the trade-off between false negative and false positive, thus minimizing the negative impact of missing values on faulty data detection. Although $I(TS,CS)$ is designed to deal with location data, it can be easily extended to other kinds of sensory data in MCS.

Through real trace-based experiments, we show that $I(TS,CS)$ can produce over 95% recall and precision in faulty data detection even when 40% of the data is missed and 40% is faulty, and the reconstruction error remains about 200 m when 30% of the data is missed and 20% is faulty.

Our major contributions are listed as follows:

- We explore the faulty data detection in MCS in a different scenario from existing works, where the sensing is sparse and multiple observations on the same object are not available.
- We design an Iterative Time Series and Compressive Sensing framework, which iteratively applies outlier detection and compressive sensing until convergence. The framework bypasses the trade-off between false positive and false negative, achieving high recall and precision at the same time.
- We evaluate $I(TS,CS)$ based on the SUVnet data set, showing its effectiveness even when 40% of the data are missing and 40% of the data are erroneous.

5.2 Problem Statement

The notation definitions are similar to that of Chap. 4. However, to take faulty data into consideration, the definitions are a bit more complicated.

We consider a location-focused MCS system consisting of n participants. Each participant uploads their location to the centralized server periodically. Time is divided into slots of duration τ (e.g., 30 s per unit), and participants upload their locations to the centralized server at each time slot, in the form of $(x(i, j), y(i, j))$ for the ith participant at the jth time slot. Considering a system operating period of t time slots, $i \in [1, n]$ and $j \in [1, t]$. Also, we assume $x(i, j)$ and $y(i, j)$ will be accurate/inaccurate/lost together.

We make the following definitions to mathematically formulate the problem.

Definition 5.1 (*Coordinate Matrices (CM)*) Describe the real locations of the participants in each time slot. We use two matrices $X_{n \times t}$ and $Y_{n \times t}$ to denote x- and y-coordinates, respectively:

$$X = [x(i, j)]_{n \times t},\qquad(5.1)$$
$$Y = [y(i, j)]_{n \times t}.\qquad(5.2)$$

This way, each line of X and Y represent a time series of location data of one participant. Note that X and Y are participants' true locations, thus containing no missing value or faulty data. Also note that all the following definitions besides Definitions 5.3, 5.5 and 5.7 have two copies for X and Y. We will only explain the X-version due to space limit.

Definition 5.2 (*Sensory Matrices (SM)*) Contain location data uploaded by participants, where faulty data or missing values may exist. SM are denoted by S_X and S_Y.

According to [18], if there is no faulty data in *SM*, it can be represented as a linear combination of *CM*:

$$S_X = \mathcal{A}(X)\qquad(5.3)$$
$$= \mathcal{E} \circ X,\qquad(5.4)$$

where $\mathcal{A}(\cdot)$ is a linear operator, and $\mathcal{E}$ is *Existence Matrix* defined as following:

Definition 5.3 (*Existence Matrix (EM)*) Is an $n \times t$ matrix, denoting if a data point in *CM* is actually collected in *SM*:

$$\mathcal{E}(i, j) = \begin{cases} 0, & \text{if } X(i, j) \text{ and } Y(i, j) \text{ are missing in SM,} \\ 1, & \text{otherwise.} \end{cases}\qquad(5.5)$$

However, when faulty data is present in the data set, the problem is no longer linear. To address this, we make the following definitions:

Definition 5.4 (*Faulty Data*) A data point $S_X(i, j)$ is faulty if the difference between $S_X(i, j)$ and $X(i, j)$, denoted by $\epsilon_{i,j}^X$, satisfies $|\epsilon_{i,j}^X| > T$, where T is a predefined threshold.

The optimal value of T is system-specific, which will be elaborated in Sect. 5.3.2.
This way, the SM can be mathematically defined as

$$S_X(i, j) = \begin{cases} 0, & \text{if } X(i, j) \text{ is missing,} \\ X(i, j) + \epsilon_{i,j}^X, & \text{otherwise,} \end{cases}\qquad(5.6)$$

where $\epsilon_{i,j}^X$s satisfy: (i) $\epsilon_{i,j}^X$ is small for normal data and large for faulty data, and (ii) the expectation of sum of $\epsilon_{i,j}^X$s in normal data $\mathbb{E}(\sum \epsilon_{i,j}^X) = 0$.

Definition 5.5 (*Faulty Matrix (FM)*) Is a matrix marking if $X(i, j)$ and $Y(i, j)$ are faulty. It is denoted by $\mathcal{F}$ and defined as

$$\mathcal{F}(i, j) = \begin{cases} 1, & \text{if } S_X(i, j) \text{ and } S_Y(i, j) \text{ are faulty} \\ 0, & \text{otherwise.} \end{cases} \tag{5.7}$$

The task of identifying the faulty data in S_X and S_Y—can be formulated as following.

Problem 5.1 (*Faulty Data Detection (FDD)*) Given S_X, S_Y and $\mathcal{E}$, find the *Detection Matrices (DM)*, denoted as $\mathcal{D}$, that is as close to $\mathcal{F}$ as possible, i.e.,

$$\begin{aligned} \text{Objective: } &\min \|\mathcal{D} - \mathcal{F}\|_F \\ \text{Subject to: } &S_X, S_Y \text{ and } \mathcal{E}, \end{aligned} \tag{5.8}$$

where $\|\cdot\|$ is the Frobenius norm quantifying the difference between $\mathcal{D}$ and $\mathcal{F}$.

To formulate the task of data reconstruction, we further make the following definitions.

Definition 5.6 (*Reconstructed Matrices (RM)*) Is generated by removing faulty data and reconstructing the missing values in S_X and S_Y. They are denoted by $\hat{X} = [\hat{x}(i, j)]_{n \times t}$ and $\hat{Y} = [\hat{y}(i, j)]_{n \times t}$.

Definition 5.7 (*Generalized Binary Index Matrix (GBIM)*) Is the combination of Existence Matrix $\mathcal{E}$ and Detection Matrix $\mathcal{D}$. It is denoted as $\mathcal{B}$ and is defined as

$$\mathcal{B}(i, j) = \begin{cases} 1, & \text{if } \mathcal{E}(i, j) = 1 \text{ and } \mathcal{D}(i, j) = 0, \\ 0, & \text{otherwise.} \end{cases} \tag{5.9}$$

This way, the task of data reconstruction can be formulated as follows:

Problem 5.2 (*Data Reconstruction (DR)*) Given S_X, S_Y and $\mathcal{B}$, determine the optimal $\hat{X}$ and $\hat{Y}$ that best approximate X and Y, i.e.,

$$\begin{aligned} \text{Objective: } &\min \|X - \hat{X}\|_F \\ \text{Subject to: } &S_X \text{ and } \mathcal{B}. \end{aligned} \tag{5.10}$$

5.3   Iterative Compressive Sensing

Below, we explain Iterative Time Series and Compressive Sensing framework $I(TS, CS)$ in detail.

Fig. 5.2 Logic flow of
I(TS,CS)

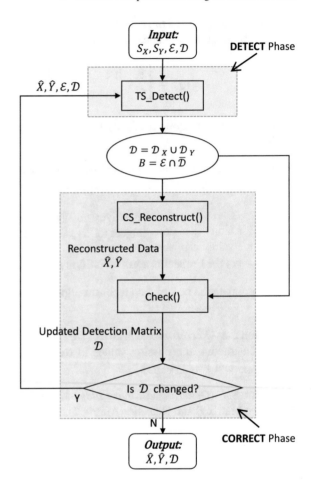

5.3.1 Overview

Intuitively, false negative and false positive are two closely coupled challenges in faulty data detection. *I(TS,CS)* mitigates such coupling with a *DETECT and COR-RECT* procedure. In the DETECT phase, *I(TS,CS)* aims to find as much faulty data as possible, even at the cost of misjudged normal data—minimizing the false negative rate at the cost of false positive. Such sacrifice on false positive is then compensated at the CORRECT phase by reconstructing the data with compressive sensing. The application of compressive sensing here is justified by (i) compressive sensing is known to reconstruct missing values effectively, and comparing to classical interpolation methods, it is relatively insensitive to the ratio of missing values [9] and (ii) the major limitation of compressive sensing—suffering from faulty data with large deviation [3]—has been mitigated during the DETECT phase.

Figure 5.2 presents an overview of the *I(TS,CS)* framework, taking *Sensory Matrices (SM)* S_X, S_Y, *Existence Matrix (EM)* $\mathcal{E}$ and *Detection Matrix (DM)* $\mathcal{D}$ as the input. In DETECT phase, *I(TS,CS)* processes the data with $TS\_Detect()$, a time series-based outlier detection algorithm, after which "suspicious" data will be detected and marked in $\mathcal{D}$. In CORRECT phase, *I(TS,CS)* treats the "suspicious" data as missing values, marks them in *Generalized Binary Index Matrix (GBIM)* B, and reconstructs them with $CS\_Reconstruct()$. Then, *I(TS,CS)* uses the *Reconstructed Matrices(RM)* $\hat{X}$, $\hat{Y}$ as ground truth to check the result of $TS\_Detect()$ and update $\mathcal{D}$. If $\mathcal{D}$ changes, *I(TS,CS)* sends the *RM*s, together with updated *DM*, *EM* and original *SM*s, back to $TS\_Detect()$. The procedure continues until $\mathcal{D}$ never changes again. The final *DM* is the set of detected faulty data.

In the rest of this section, we will introduce the detailed design of $TS\_Detect()$, $CS\_Reconstruct()$ and $Check()$. Specifically, we designed optimized local median method for faulty data detecting and checking, and modified Compressive Sensing for missing value reconstruction.

5.3.2 Optimized Local Median Method

Optimized Local Median Method is a variant of outlier detection method in time series. Here, we use outliers and faulty data interchangeably—neither of them can be used by the MCS system and thus are *faulty* in our focus.

Figure 5.3 illustrates the main idea of the Local Median Method. We select the ith row of the sensory matrix S_X (or S_Y), denoted as $\mathbf{x_i} = [x_i^{(1)}, x_i^{(2)}, \ldots, x_i^{(t)}]$, and test the data points one by one. Define an odd window size w. When testing $x_i^{(k)}$, we consider the $(w - 1)$ points around $x_i^{(k)}$, i.e., $[x_i^{(l)}, \ldots, x_i^{(k)}, \ldots, x_i^{(l+w-1)}]$, and calculate the median of these w values, denoted by $m^{(k)}$. Note that l is the index of the first time slot in the window, as defined in Eq. (5.12). The tested data $x_i^{(k)}$ is judged as faulty if $|x_i^{(k)} - m^{(k)}| > \delta$, where δ is a tolerance threshold.

Predefining a fixed δ for the Local Median Method does not work well for location data. For example, vehicles on a highway may run at 100 km/h, but only at 20 km/h on local road. Assuming $\tau = 30$ s, the maximum distance a vehicle can run in a time slot is 833 m in the former case, but is only 167 m in the latter—a data point with 300 m deviation from median will be normal in the highway scenario but is likely faulty on local road.

We use velocity, i.e., the changing rate of location, to optimize the setting of δ, which is readily available on many mobile systems such as vehicles and smartphones. The velocities are represented by two matrices $V_x = [v_x(i, j)]_{n \times t}$ and $V_y = [v_y(i, j)]_{n \times t}$, where $v_x(i, j)$ and $v_y(i, j)$ represent the velocity component in X and Y direction of the ith participant in the jth time slot, respectively.

We estimate how far a participant could travel within one time slot based on his velocity. However, $v_x(i, j)$s and $v_y(i, j)$s are instant velocities at exactly the time when location is collected, and thus may not capture the average velocity within a

Fig. 5.3 Local median method

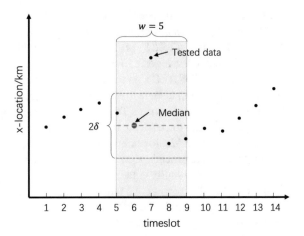

time slot accurately. As a remedy, we define Average Velocity Matrices $\overline{V}_x$ and $\overline{V}_y$ as

$$\overline{V}_x = \begin{bmatrix} v_x(1,1) & \frac{v_x(1,1)+v_x(1,2)}{2} & \cdots & \frac{v_x(1,t-1)+v_x(1,t)}{2} \\ v_x(2,1) & \frac{v_x(2,1)+v_x(2,2)}{2} & \cdots & \frac{v_x(2,t-1)+v_x(2,t)}{2} \\ \vdots & \vdots & & \vdots \\ v_x(n,1) & \frac{v_x(n,1)+v_x(n,2)}{2} & \cdots & \frac{v_x(n,t-1)+v_x(n,t)}{2} \end{bmatrix}. \tag{5.11}$$

and $\overline{V}_y$ is defined similarly. We then apply linear interpolation to estimate the average velocity based on $\overline{V}_x$ and $\overline{V}_y$. Denote $\overline{V}_x(i, j)$ as the average X direction velocity component of the ith participant from the $(j - 1)$th to jth time slot. For simplicity, we assume $v_x(i, 0) = v_x(i, 1)$ and $v_y(i, 0) = v_y(i, 1)$, i.e., the average velocity from the zeroth and the first time slot is instant velocity of the first time slot.

We define the dynamic tolerance δ based on the maximum distance a participant can travel within w time slots. Specifically, the tolerance of the ith participant, jth time slot, in X direction is defined as

$$\delta_i^{(j)} = \xi \times \max_{k=1,2,\ldots,w} \{\sum_{p=l}^{l+k} \overline{V}_x(i, j) \times \tau\}, \tag{5.12}$$

$$l = \min\{\max\{1, j - (w - 1)/2\}, t - w + 1\},$$

where l is the index of the first time slot in the window, τ is the length of each time slot, and ξ is a parameter to fine-tune the trade-off between false negative and false positive errors.

Note that we ignore missing values in the Local Median Method—if there are n missing values in the window, we calculate median $m^{(j)}$ and $\delta_i^{(j)}$ based on the remaining $(w - n)$ data points. Such simplification may reduce the reliability of the faulty data detection method, which can be compensated in the CHECK phase, as we will explain later.

Algorithm 5.1 shows the pseudo code of the Optimized Local Median Method. First, the first three input of $TS\_Detect()$ can be either X-Version or Y-Version. The returned $\mathcal{D}$ is also either $\mathcal{D}_X$ or $\mathcal{D}_Y$. The final DM is $\mathcal{D} = \mathcal{D}_X \cup \mathcal{D}_Y$ (see Fig. 5.2). Second, $\mathcal{D}$ is set to all ones when $TS\_Detect()$ is executed for the first time, and its corresponding element will be set to 0 if a data point is concluded to be normal. This is because $TS\_Detect()$ is designed to find as much faulty data as possible, regardless of how many normal data are misjudged. Moreover, this ensures the convergence of the $I(TS,CS)$ framework. Third, missing values appear in $TS\_Detect()$ only when it is first executed, and will be replaced by the reconstructed value after reconstructing the data set.

Algorithm 5.1: TS_Detect($S,\hat{S},\overline{V},D,\mathcal{E},w,\xi$)

Input : Sensory Matrix S; Reconstructed Matrix $\hat{S}$; Average Velocity Matrix $\overline{V}$; Detection Matrix $\mathcal{D}$; Existence Matrix $\mathcal{E}$; Window Size w; Trade-off Coefficient ξ

Output: Faulty data detection result $\mathcal{D}$

1   **if** *Not first executed* **then**
2   **foreach** $S(i, j)$ **do**
3   **if** $\mathcal{E}(i, j) = 0$ **then**
4         $S(i, j) \leftarrow \hat{S}(i, j)$;

5     $\mathcal{E} \leftarrow ones(n, t)$;

6   **for** $i \leftarrow 1$ *to* n **do**
7   **for** $j \leftarrow 1$ *to* t **do**
8   **if** $\mathcal{E}(i, j) = 0$ **then**
9   **continue**;
10   Calculate l and δ according to Eq. (5.12);
11      $N \leftarrow \emptyset$;
12   **for** $k \leftarrow l$ *to* $l + w - 1$ **do**
13   **if** $\mathcal{E}(i, k) = 1$ **then**
14   Add $S(i, j)$ to N;
15      $m \leftarrow$ median of N;
16   **if** $|S(i, j) - m| < \delta$ **then**
17        $\mathcal{D}(i, j) \leftarrow 0$;

18 **return** $\mathcal{D}$;

5.3.3 Time Series and Compressive Sensing

The improvement of compressive sensing has been discussed in Sect. 4.5. Here, we will omit the exploration of low-rank structure and the derivation of original compressive sensing, and directly show an improvement that is specially designed for location data.

5.3.3.1 Temporal Stability and Velocity Improvement

From Sect. 3.3.4, we know that the original compressive sensing problem can be summarized by the following optimization problem:

$$\min(\|(LR^T) \circ \mathcal{B}_X - S_X\|_F^2 + \lambda_1(\|L\|_F^2 + \|R\|_F^2)), \tag{5.13}$$

where λ_1 is a parameter for tuning the trade-off between rank minimization and fitting accuracy.

Next, we will introduce additional information—temporal information and velocity information—into it to improve the recovery accuracy.

We first consider the temporal stability property. In real world, most environmental value tends to be stable between adjacent time slots when the interval is not too large. We measure the temporal stability of participant i at time slot j by calculating the difference between adjacent time slots

$$\triangle x(i, j) = |x(i, j) - x(i, j-1)|, \tag{5.14}$$

and $\triangle y(i, j)$ is defined similarly.

We can introduce temporal stability into compressive sensing by adding the summation of $\triangle x(i, j)$ into object function (5.13). Theoretically, the smaller $\triangle x(i, j)$ is, the more accurate the result is. Thus, we may incorporate velocity to further extract temporal stability property. The rationale of the design is that the estimated average velocity times the time slot duration τ should be approximately equal to the distance traveled in the time slot. We measure "velocity improved temporal stability" of participant i at time slot j by

$$\triangle_v x(i, j) = |x(i, j) - x(i, j-1)| - \overline{V}_x(i, j) \times \tau, \tag{5.15}$$

where $\overline{V}_x$ is Average Velocity Matrix defined by Eq. (5.11) and τ is time slot duration.

Figure 5.4b shows the CDF of $\triangle x$, $\triangle y$, $\triangle_v x$ and $\triangle_v y$. The x-axis represents the normalized difference between two consecutive time slots in Coordinate Matrices, and the y-axis represents the cumulative probability. In the figure, we see that before incorporating velocity, 95% of $\triangle x(i, j)$s are less than 410 m, which is reduced to 210 m by incorporating velocity.

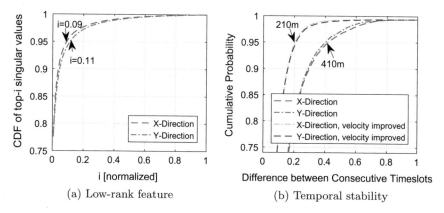

Fig. 5.4 Features extracted from selected data set

After incorporating velocity-improved temporal constraint, the minimization problem (5.13) changes into:

$$\min(\|(LR^T) \circ \mathcal{B}_X - S_X\|_F^2 + \lambda_1(\|L\|_F^2 + \|R\|_F^2) \\ + \lambda_2 \|LR^T\mathbb{T} - \tau\overline{V}_x\|_F^2, \tag{5.16}$$

where $\overline{V}_x$ is average velocity matrix defined in Eq. (5.11), τ is time slot duration, and

$$\mathbb{T} = \begin{bmatrix} 1 & -1 & 0 & \dots & 0 \\ 0 & 1 & -1 & \ddots & \vdots \\ 0 & 0 & 1 & \ddots & 0 \\ \vdots & \vdots & \ddots & \ddots & -1 \\ 0 & 0 & \dots & 0 & 1 \end{bmatrix}_{t \times t}. \tag{5.17}$$

The matrix $LR^T\mathbb{T}$ captures time stability of the data set, and $\tau\overline{V}_X$ incorporates velocity. Note that temporal stability is an intrinsic property of location data, and velocity is closely related to location, but collected from another dimension. Thereby, the additional constraint provides more information and can filter out more noises.

5.3.3.2 Modified CS Algorithm

The Modified CS algorithm finds the appropriate L and R that minimize (5.16). We define the object function

$$f(L, R) = f_1(L, R) + f_2(L, R) + f_3(L, R), \tag{5.18}$$

where

$$f_1(L, R) = \|(LR^T) \circ \mathcal{B}_X - S_X\|_F^2,   \qquad (5.19)$$

$$f_2(L, R) = \lambda_1(\|L\|_F^2 + \|R\|_F^2),   \qquad (5.20)$$

$$f_3(L, R) = \lambda_2\|LR^T\mathbb{T} - \tau\overline{V}_x\|_F^2.   \qquad (5.21)$$

Obviously, (5.18) is non-convex. However, if we fix L or R, the other would be convex. Thus, we apply Alternating Steepest Descent (ASD) algorithm [14, 16], which has been proved to be efficient for minimization problem. The main idea of ASD is to alternatively perform steepest gradient descend on L and R. First, L and R are randomly initialized. Note the parameter r is the estimated rank of X, which can be determined by experiment. Next, we iteratively fix L and perform gradient descent on R, and fix R and perform gradient descent on L. The steepest descent along R and L are selected to minimize the updated value of f along the direction ∇_r and ∇_l, respectively. This can be solved by calculating the differential of f and set it to zero, i.e., assume $g_r(\alpha) = f(R, R - \alpha\nabla_r)$, $g_l(\alpha) = f(L, L - \alpha\nabla_l)$, let $g_r'(\alpha) = g_l'(\alpha) = 0$, and solve α.

Algorithm 5.2: CS_Reconstruct($S,\mathcal{B},\overline{V},\lambda_1,\lambda_2,r,ratio$)

Input : Sensory Matrix S; Generalized Binary Index Matrix $\mathcal{B}$; Average Velocity Matrix $\overline{V}$;
             Trade-off Coefficient λ_1, λ_2; Rank bound r; Terminate Ratio $ratio$
Output: Reconstructed Matrix $\hat{S}$

1 $m, n \leftarrow size(S)$;
2 $S' \leftarrow S$;
3 **foreach** $S'(i, j)$ *in* S' **do**
4 | **if** $\mathcal{B}(i, j) = 0$ **then**
5 | $\lfloor$ $S'(i, j) \leftarrow$ the nearest existing value;

6 $[U, \Sigma, V] \leftarrow svd(S')$;
7 $L \leftarrow U * \Sigma_r^{1/2}$;   /* The first r cols of Σ */
8 $R \leftarrow V * (\Sigma_r^T)^{1/2}$ /* The first r rows of Σ */
9 **repeat**
10 | $\mu_1 \leftarrow f(L, R)$;
11 | $\nabla_r \leftarrow \frac{\partial f(L,R)}{\partial R}$;
12 | $\alpha_r \leftarrow \arg\min_\alpha f(L, R - \alpha\nabla_r)$;
13 | $R \leftarrow R - \alpha_r\nabla_r$;
14 | $\nabla_l \leftarrow \frac{\partial f(L,R)}{\partial L}$;
15 | $\alpha_l \leftarrow \arg\min_\alpha f(L, L - \alpha\nabla_l)$;
16 | $L \leftarrow L - \alpha_l\nabla_r$;
17 | $\mu_2 \leftarrow f(L, R)$;
18 **until** $\frac{\mu_2-\mu_1}{\mu_1} < ratio$;
19 $\hat{S} \leftarrow L * R^T$;
20 **return** $\hat{S}$;

Algorithm 5.3: Check($S,\hat{S},\mathcal{D},thres_l,thres_h$)

Input : Sensory Matrix S; Reconstructed Matrix $\hat{S}$; Detection Matrix $\mathcal{D}$; Threshold $thres_l$, $thres_u$;
Output: Updated Faulty Data Detection Matrix $\mathcal{D}$
1 **foreach** $S(i, j)$ *in* S **do**
2   **if** $|S(i, j) - \hat{S}(i, j)| < thres_l$ and $\mathcal{D}(i, j) = 1$ **then**
3          $\mathcal{D}(i, j) \leftarrow 0$;
4   **if** $|S(i, j) - \hat{S}(i, j)| > thres_u$ and $\mathcal{D}(i, j) = 0$ **then**
5          $\mathcal{D}(i, j) \leftarrow 1$;

6 **return** $\mathcal{D}$;

ASD might suffer from local optimal in practice. To mitigate it, we optimize the initial value of R and L by: (i) letting $S' = S$ and the missing values in S' be its nearest existing value; intuitively, S' is approximate to the original *Coordinate Matrix (CM)*; (ii) applying SVD to S' and computing R and L. This way, starting points of R and L are close to the optimal one, and thus alleviates the potential local-optimal problem. The pseudo code of modified CS is shown in Algorithm 5.2.

Check() compares the original *SM*s to *RM*s: if the difference is less than a lower threshold while the corresponding element in D is 1, turn it to 0; if the difference is larger than a upper threshold while the corresponding element in D is 0, turn it to 1. Similar to Algorithm 5.1, this algorithm also has X-Version and Y-Version, whose pseudo code is summarized in Algorithm 5.3.

5.3.4 Discussion

The overall time complexity of $I(TS,CS)$ framework is $N(O(TS\_Detect) + O(CS\_Reconstruct) + O(Check))$, where N is the number of iterations. $O(TS\_Detect) = O(ntw) = O(nt)$ and $O(Check) = O(nt)$. The computational cost of $O(CS\_Reconstruct)$ is dominated by a series of matrix multiplications, which is $O(mnt)$, where m is the iteration time in ASD algorithm. As a result, the total complexity of $I(TS,CS)$ is $O(Nmnt)$.

In the design of $I(TS,CS)$, velocity plays an important part. It seems that if the velocity data itself is faulty and contains missing values, the performance of $I(TS,CS)$ framework will be impacted. In fact, this impact is negligible. This is proved in Sect. 5.4.4.

5.4　Evaluation

In this section, we evaluate $I(TS,CS)$ in terms of faulty data detection performance and data reconstruction accuracy.

5.4.1　Evaluation Settings

We evaluate $I(TS,CS)$ based on the taxi data in SUVnet [1]. In the evaluation, we selected a trace containing 158 participants × 240 time slots, with slot duration $\tau = 30$ s. The original data is stored in two matrices $X_{n \times t}$ and $Y_{n \times t}$. The spatial size of the taxi data is 110 × 140 km, covering major area of Shanghai.

In the trace-driven evaluation, the Existence Matrix $\mathcal{E}$ is randomly generated with a control parameter α specifying the ratio of 0s (i.e., missing values) in $\mathcal{E}$. Also, we randomly select a fraction of the data set as faulty data. These points are marked in the Faulty Matrix F by setting the corresponding element to be 1. The ratio of faulty data is controlled by β. For the faulty data, we add a random bias $\epsilon_{i,j}$ to the original data, i.e., the generated Sensory Matrices are $S_X = X \circ \mathcal{E} + \mathcal{F} \circ [\epsilon_{i,j}]_{n \times t}$ and $S_Y = Y \circ \mathcal{E} + \mathcal{F} \circ [\epsilon_{i,j}]_{n \times t}$.

We evaluate the performance in two aspects: performance in faulty data detection and performance in reconstruction error. The performance in faulty data detection is judged by precision and recall, which are defined as $Precision = \frac{\#TP}{\#TP + \#FP}$ and $Recall = \frac{\#TP}{\#TP + \#FN}$, where $\#TP, \#FP$ and $\#FN$ represent True Positive (concluded as faulty data and is indeed faulty data), False Positive (concluded as faulty data while actually is not faulty data), and False Negative (not concluded as faulty data while actually is faulty data), respectively.

The accuracy of missing value reconstruction is measured by *Mean Absolute Error (MAE)*

$$err = \frac{\sum_{i,j:\mathcal{E}(i,j)=0 \ or \ \mathcal{D}(i,j)=1} \sqrt{err_x(i,j)^2 + err_y(i,j)^2}}{\sum_{i,j:\mathcal{E}(i,j)=0 \ or \ \mathcal{D}(i,j)=1} 1}, \qquad (5.22)$$

where

$$err_x(i,j) = |X(i,j) - \hat{X}(i,j)|, \qquad (5.23)$$
$$err_y(i,j) = |Y(i,j) - \hat{Y}(i,j)|. \qquad (5.24)$$

We use the following three methods as benchmarks when evaluating the performance in faulty data detection:

- *Two-sided median method (TMM)*: A time series-based outlier detection algorithm proposed in [2], which also compares each data points with the median in the window, but the outlier range is predefined;

- *I(TS,CS) without VT*: Similar to *I(TS,CS)*, but the compressive sensing is not temporal and velocity improved;
- *I(TS,CS) without V*: Similar to *I(TS,CS)*, the compressive sensing is temporal improved but not velocity improved.

Because TMM does not provide data reconstruction, when evaluating the reconstruction error, we replace it with the following method:

- *Modified compressive sensing*: The algorithm is described in Sect. 5.3.3.

5.4.2 Performance in Faulty Data Detection

We first evaluate the performance of faulty data detection in terms of precision and recall. The experiment is conducted when missing value ratio $\alpha = 0$, 20 and 40%, and in each experiment the faulty data ratio β varies from 10 to 40%. The results are shown in Fig. 5.5.

When missing value ratio $\alpha = 0\%$ (Fig. 5.5a, c, e and faulty data ratio β is low ($\leq 20\%$), all these four methods produce similar precision and recall ($>98\%$). However, with β continuing raising, the precision and recall of TMM drops while that of the other three methods remains high. When $\alpha = 0\%$, precision and recall of time series-based method drops to 91% and 96%, respectively, while that of the other three methods is still more than 98%. This indicates that $I(TS,CS)$ improves faulty data detection even in case of no missing value.

When $\alpha > 0\%$, even if β is low, there is still a distinct gap between the performance of TMM and the other three methods. We can observe that the performance of the three $I(TS,CS)$-like methods is very stable. Even when the data quality is quite bad, i.e., with $\alpha = 40\%$ and $\beta = 40\%$, the precision and recall is still more than 95%.

Note that the precision and recall of the three $I(TS,CS)$-like methods are almost indistinguishable. This is because the faulty data is typically at least kilometers away from the normal data. However, as we will see later, the reconstruction error of all these three $I(TS,CS)$-like methods is less than 1 km in most cases. Consequently, the difference in reconstruction error among the three $I(TS,CS)$-like methods can hardly influence the performance of faulty data detection.

5.4.3 Performance in Missing Value Reconstruction

In this section, we evaluate $I(TS,CS)$'s reconstruction error. The experiment is conducted when missing value ratio $\alpha = 10$, 20 and 30%, and in each experiment, the faulty data ratio β varies from 0 to 40%. The results are shown in Fig. 5.6. When there is no faulty data ($\beta = 0\%$), the reconstruction error of CS is slightly less than those of the three $I(TS,CS)$-like method. That is because in $I(TS,CS)$, the DETECT phase will introduce misjudged "faulty data", and increase the overall missing value ratio.

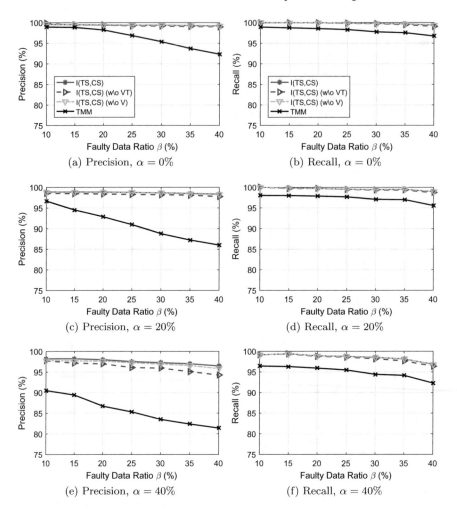

Fig. 5.5 Performance of faulty data detection

However, the difference between reconstruction of CS and other three *I(TS,CS)*-like methods decreases when more values are missing.

Faulty data, even if only 5% of the total volume, increases CS's reconstruction error dramatically. In contrast, the reconstruction error of the other three *I(TS,CS)*-like methods does not change a lot. When $\beta = 40\%$, CS's reconstruction error increases to over 1200 m, while that of *I(TS,CS)* remains at about 200 m. *I(TS,CS)* performs the best among the three *I(TS,CS)*-like methods. Specifically, the reconstruction error of *I(TS,CS)* is only half of that with *I(TS,CS)* without VT, and about 10–18% better than *I(TS,CS)* without V. In most cases ($\beta \leq 30\%$, $\alpha \leq 20\%$), the reconstruction error of *I(TS,CS)* is less than 200 m. Even when there 30% of the data is missing and 40% of the data is faulty, the reconstruction error is still less than 300 m. Compared to

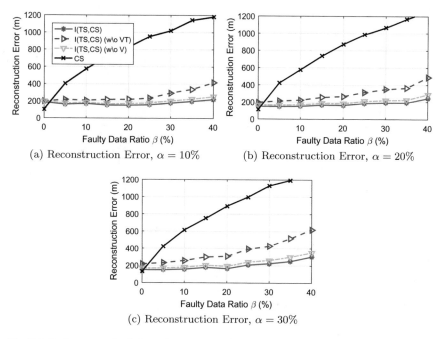

Fig. 5.6 Performance of missing value reconstruction

spatial size of the traces (110×140 km), the error is acceptable. Such errors can be further reduced via map matching [7, 15].

5.4.4 Impact of Faulty and Missing Data in Velocity

In this section, we evaluate the impact of faulty data in velocity. In the experiment, we randomly select a fraction (noted by γ) of velocity data set, and artificially add 100% error onto it (i.e., suppose the original velocity is v, the modified velocity with error is randomly selected between 0 to $2v$). From Sect. 5.5, we know that the recall and precision does not show much difference between the three $I(TS,CS)$-like methods. Thus, we only compare the reconstruction error between $I(TS,CS)$ with faulty velocity and $I(TS,CS)$ without V.

The results are shown in Fig. 5.7. The experiment is conducted when missing value ratio $\alpha = 20$ and 40%, and the faulty data ratio varies from 10 to 40%. We can observe that when 20% of the velocity is faulty, the reconstruction error is almost the same as that when no faulty data exists in velocity. Even when 40% of the velocity is faulty, the reconstruction error only slightly increases. In contrast, if velocity is not utilized, the reconstruction error dramatically increases.

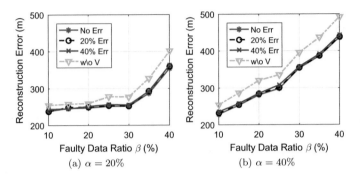

Fig. 5.7 Impact of velocity faulty data

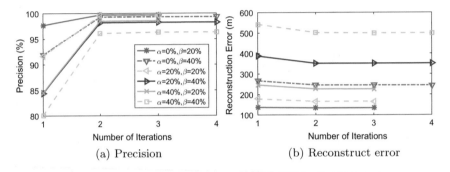

Fig. 5.8 Converging rate of $I(TS,CS)$

5.4.5   Convergence

Last but not the least, we evaluate $I(TS,CS)$'s converging rate. The precision and reconstruction error in each iterations are shown in Fig. 5.8. Under all circumstances, the improvement between iteration 1 and iteration 2 is significant, and the later iterations only contribute tiny improvement. Moreover, $I(TS,CS)$ converges in no more than 4 iterations even when $\alpha = 40\%$ and $\beta = 40\%$.

5.5   Summary

In this chapter, we focused on location data in mobile crowdsensing and considered the problem of faulty data detection in the presence of missing values. We learned $I(TS,CS)$ framework in which time series-based outlier detection method and compressive sensing are iteratively conducted. We further improve the performance of $I(TS,CS)$ by modifying compressive sensing and having the outlier region of time series-based outlier detection method dynamically calculated. Finally, we conduct a real trace-based evaluation, showing that $I(TS,CS)$ framework can drastically improve the performance of faulty data detection and missing value reconstruction.

References

1. (2007) SUVnet data collected by Shanghai Jiao Tong University. http://wirelesslab.sjtu.edu.cn/download.html
2. Basu S, Meckesheimer M (2007) Automatic outlier detection for time series: an application to sensor data. Knowl Inf Syst (KIS) 11(2):137–154
3. Candes EJ, Plan Y (2010) Matrix completion with noise. Proc IEEE 98(6):925–936
4. Chen Y, Qiu L, Guangtao X, Hu Z (2014) Robust network compressive sensing. In: International conference on mobile computing and networking (MOBICOM), ACM, pp 545–556
5. Du Y, Sun YE, Huang H, Huang L, Xu H, Bao Y, Guo H (2019) Bayesian co-clustering truth discovery for mobile crowd sensing systems. IEEE Trans Ind Inform
6. Fox AJ (1972) Outliers in time series. J R Stat Soc Ser B (Methodol), pp 350–363
7. Gong YJ, Chen E, Zhang X, Ni LM, Zhang J (2018) Antmapper: an ant colony-based map matching approach for trajectory-based applications. IEEE Trans Intell Transp Syst 19(2):390–401
8. Jin H, Su L, Xiao H, Nahrstedt K (2016) Inception: incentivizing privacy-preserving data aggregation for mobile crowd sensing systems. In: International symposium on mobile Ad Hoc networking and computing (MobiHoc), ACM/IEEE, pp 341–350
9. Kong L, Xia M, Liu XY, Wu MY, Liu X (2013) Data loss and reconstruction in sensor networks. In: International conference on computer communications (INFOCOM), IEEE, pp 1654–1662
10. Li Y, Li Q, Gao J, Su L, Zhao B, Fan W, Han J (2015) On the discovery of evolving truth. In: Knowledge discovery and data mining (SIGKDD), ACM, pp 675–684
11. Meng C, Jiang W, Li Y, Gao J, Su L, Ding H, Cheng Y (2015) Truth discovery on crowd sensing of correlated entities. In: Knowledge discovery and data mining (SenSys), ACM, pp 169–182
12. Nie J, Luo J, Xiong Z, Niyato D, Wang P (2019) A stackelberg game approach toward socially-aware incentive mechanisms for mobile crowdsensing. IEEE Trans Wirel Commun 18(1):724–738
13. Saroiu S, Wolman A (2010) I am a sensor, and I approve this message. In: Workshop on mobile computing systems & applications, pp 37–42
14. Tanner J, Wei K (2016) Low rank matrix completion by alternating steepest descent methods. Appl Comput Harmon Anal 40(2):417–429
15. White CE, Bernstein D, Kornhauser AL (2000) Some map matching algorithms for personal navigation assistants. Transp Res Part C Emerg Technol 8(1):91–108
16. Wu F, Liu D, Wu Z, Zhang Y, Chen G (2017) Cost-efficient indoor white space exploration through compressive sensing. Trans Netw (ToN)
17. Yang S, Wu F, Tang S, Gao X, Yang B, Chen G (2017) On designing data quality-aware truth estimation and surplus sharing method for mobile crowdsensing. J Sel Areas Commun (JSAC) 35(4):832–847
18. Zhang Y, Roughan M, Willinger W, Qiu L (2009) Spatio-temporal compressive sensing and internet traffic matrices. In: International conference on the applications, technologies, architectures, and protocols for computer communication (Signcomm), ACM, pp 1–1
19. Zheng Y, Duan H, Wang C (2018) Learning the truth privately and confidently: encrypted confidence-aware truth discovery in mobile crowdsensing. IEEE Trans Inf Forensics Secur 13(10):2475–2489

Chapter 6
Homogeneous Compressive Sensing for Privacy Preservation

From Chaps. 4 and 5, we have learnt how compressive sensing and its extended versions effectively reconstruct incomplete data set and help tackling the data quality maintenance problem in MCS. In this chapter, we will turn around and see a new topic: privacy preservation problem. The key problem of this chapter is how to preserve the privacy without impacting the accuracy of data reconstruction. This problem is important because most participators would like to contribute in mobile crowdsensing at least their privacy can be protected. Next, we will first have a glance at the background of location-based services and privacy preservation. Then, the problem of privacy preservation in incomplete data set is mathematically modeled and the homogeneous compressive sensing based privacy preservation scheme, *PPCS*, is introduced, followed by the theoretical analysis of the effectiveness of the new-designed scheme.

6.1 Background

Location-based services (LBSs) [6, 17, 32] have experienced an explosive growth recently, which are evolving from utilizing a single location [8] to harness the complete trajectory of a mobile user [11, 19, 34]. For example, the Moves application, which automatically tracks both activities and trajectories of users, has been downloaded over 4 million times since its launch in January 2013 and has been acquired by Facebook [4].

This chapter is represented with permission from ©[2015] IEEE ref. Kong, L., He, L., Liu, X.Y., Gu, Y., Wu, M.Y. and Liu, X., 2015, June. Privacy-preserving compressive sensing for crowdsensing based trajectory recovery. In *IEEE 35th International Conference on Distributed Computing Systems* (pp. 31–40).

© Springer Nature Singapore Pte Ltd. 2019
L. Kong et al., *When Compressive Sensing Meets Mobile Crowdsensing*, https://doi.org/10.1007/978-981-13-7776-1_6

Although GPS is universally available on modern devices, the trajectory of a mobile user may always be incomplete due to none-line-of-sight to satellites [23]. In addition, since GPS consumes a significant amount of energy, it is only activated periodically to conserve energy [18]. Consequently, the trajectory recovery [24] is one of the fundamental components of LBSs to estimate the missing data in an incomplete trajectory. For instance, trippermap [1] in Flickr can automatically reproduce a user's traveling path based on her geotagged photos.

Considerable interpolation methods have been devoted to trajectory recovery. With a single user's incomplete trajectory data, the methods such as nearest neighbors [25] and linear interpolation [30] can attain only coarse-grained accuracy. More recently, Rallapalli et al. [23] reveal that the trajectories of multiple users within the same geographic area are strongly correlated. For instance, students in the same campus have similar time tables; vehicles in the same segment of freeway moves with similar velocities. Leveraging such correlations, the crowdsensing technology provides a promising recovery method, which collectively recovers all users' trajectories together using Compressive Sensing (CS). This crowdsensing recovery method is proved to be superior to interpolation methods with only single user data [23].

While the crowdsensing recovery method accomplishes the better accuracy, the major drawback for applying it in practice is its requirement to collect all users' location data, which poses great concerns for potential privacy leakage [26, 31]. Especially in crowdsensing, the users are willing to contribute their personal data only when their privacies are preserved. Currently, the most commonly adopted privacy-preserving approach is anonymization [20]. Nevertheless, the latest studies [10, 33] reveal that the anonymization mechanism alone is inadequate. To further improve the privacy, dummification [16] and obfuscation [13, 15, 22] methods are introduced, which inject fake trajectories and perturb original trajectories, respectively. Although dummification and obfuscation methods reasonably protect user privacies, they also pollute the original data, which decreases the recovery accuracy with current crowdsensing recovery method.

6.2 Problem Statement

In this section, we introduce the trajectory recovery model, the adversary model, and the formal definition of our problem.

6.2.1 Trajectory Recovery Model

A trajectory is composed of a sequence of locations that a user traverses, represented by her corresponding longitude x and latitude y, as shown in Fig. 6.1a. The user's current location (x, y) can be obtained through the GPS module on her mobile device. In an N-user system where the total duration of interests consist of T time slots, the

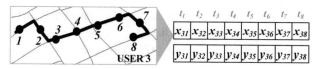

(a) Two vectors are used to record the longitude x and the latitude y data of a user's trajectory, whose ID is 3.

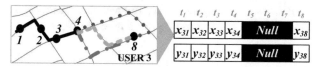

(b) When some location data are missing, the corresponding elements in the vectors are null. It is not easy to directly recover the accurate trajectory due to several possible paths in map.

Fig. 6.1 Trajectory model

trajectory of the ith user is represented by two $1 \times T$ vectors, where x_{ij} and y_{ij} are the longitude and latitude at the jth time slot respectively ($i = 1, 2, \ldots, N$ and $j = 1, 2, \ldots, T$).

The location data of a user could be partially missing due to reasons such as none line of sight to GPS satellites, energy management of GPS module on mobile devices [18, 28], and so on. In Fig. 6.1b, the null elements in the vectors indicate the data missing at their corresponding time slots.

The trajectory recovery is not effective if it is performed for individual users independently. For example, as shown in Fig. 6.1b, the location data for the fifth to seventh time slots are missing. Even though the map matching [27] method is utilized to narrow down the field of candidates, there are still three possible trajectories provided by linear interpolation [25]. To address the weakness of the single user recovery, the crowdsensing recovery exploits the correlation among users and recovers all users' trajectories together using compressive sensing, which is verified to outperform existing methods [23] and is referred to as the state of the art.

The notations of the crowdsensing recovery are defined as:

- *Trajectory Matrix* is a set of N users' actual trajectories, which is defined as $X = (x_{ij})_{N \times T}$. We only illustrate the longitude X related definitions and derivations in the following sections. All results for the latitude Y are similar to X, which are omitted for conciseness.
- *Binary Index Matrix* is used to indicate whether a location data in X is missing, which is defined as

$$\Phi = (\phi_{i,j})_{N \times T} = \begin{cases} 0 \text{ if } x_{i,j} \text{ is missing,} \\ 1 \text{ otherwise.} \end{cases} \tag{6.1}$$

- *Sensed Matrix* consists of the sensed location data from GPS. Due to the potential data missing, elements in the sensed matrix S are either x_{ij} (i.e., sensed location data) or 0 (i.e., missing data). Thus, S can be presented by

$$S = X \circ \Phi. \tag{6.2}$$

- *Recovered Matrix* is generated by recovering the missing data in the sensed matrix S to approximate the actual trajectories X. The recovered matrix is denoted by $\hat{X}$.
- *Compressive Sensing* (CS). We use fcs to denote the CS operation, thus $\hat{X} = fcs(S)$.

6.2.2   User Models and Adversary Models

We consider a system consisting of two types of mobile users: public and private users. Public users are willing to share their trajectories and private users want to avoid the exposure of their trajectories. For example, in an urban traffic scenario, buses can be treated as public users, and personal vehicles are good examples of private users.

As leakage of personal trajectories can lead to unauthorized surveillance and tracking, adversaries are motivated to obtain private users' trajectories. In Fig. 6.2, we illustrate the adversary models that threaten the privacy in crowdsensing recovery, which are categorized as eavesdroppers, hackers, and stalkers.

- *Eavesdroppers and hackers*: An eavesdropper could capture the data traffic between users and the crowdsensing server by hijacking the communication channels. A hacker could access and obtain all data in the server. Because eavesdroppers and hackers can obtain the same set of information, we do not differentiate them in the rest of this chapter.
- *Stalkers*: A stalker can track a user for a short while and obtain k actual location data of that user. Without loss of generality, we assume that k is a small number compared with the total number of data in a complete trajectory, because a stalker cannot always tail after the user.

Fig. 6.2 Adversary models

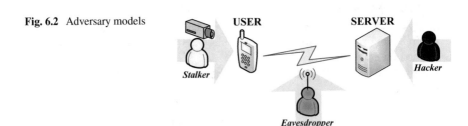

All adversaries potentially have the following capabilities: (i) they have the same algorithms as ours to recover the trajectory; (ii) they can exploit existing map matching methods [21, 27] as ours to further improve their estimation accuracy.

6.2.3 Accuracy and Privacy Problem

In this chapter, we consider the *accurate* and *privacy-preserving* trajectory recovery problem. This problem is challenging because the two objectives appear to be conflicted with each other. On one hand, a highly accurate recovery can be achieved by the crowdsensing method. However, this method requires to collect data from all users, which poses the potential privacy leakage. On the other hand, the privacy objective is to avoid the exposure of users' trajectories, which is contrary to the basic requirement of crowdsensing. Existing methods cannot satisfy the two objectives simultaneously.

To address this dilemma in crowdsensing based trajectory recovery, we propose the *PPCS* scheme, in which a novel homomorphic obfuscation method for CS is designed to preserve the user privacy and guarantee the recovery accuracy as well.

6.3 Homogeneous Compressive Sensing Scheme

To address the privacy issue in conventional CS, we present a simple but efficient trajectory recovery scheme *Privacy-Preserving Compressive Sensing* (PPCS) in this section.

6.3.1 Trace Preparation and Validation

Before describing the design of PPCS scheme, we introduce two real traces and validate their low-rank properties, which implies the strong correlation among multiple users' trajectories within the same area [23].

6.3.1.1 Preprocessing of Real-World Mobility Traces

The evaluation of our design is based on two publicly available mobility traces: Geolife [3] and SUVnet [2]. These two traces have large amount of users, long durations, and mixed mobility modes. Geolife records the GPS trajectories of 178 users from April 2007 to October 2011 in Beijing, in which the major user mobility modes include walking, biking, and driving. SUVnet records the trajectories of over 2000 taxis and 300 buses in the urban area of Shanghai.

Table 6.1 Recovery error when stalkers have partial original data

Name	Size	Area (km^2)	Mobility mode
Beijing	116 users × 355 slots	70 × 85	Walk/Bike/Car
Shanghai	74 users × 399 slots	100 × 100	Taxi/Bus

However, the raw traces from Geolife and SUVnet cannot be directly utilized for low-rank validation, because a significant amount of their data are missing. To guarantee the integrity of ground truth, we perform trace preprocessing on the raw data to select their complete subsets and build the trajectory matrices, which are then utilized in our evaluations. The description of the two selected traces including their sizes, areas, mobility modes are shown in Table 6.1, which are denoted as Beijing and Shanghai, respectively.

6.3.1.2 Validating the Low-Rank Property

As CS is a major component of PPCS, we first need to validate whether the trajectory matrices are low rank, which is the requirement for the CS operation.

Although the low-rank property has been studied in [23], each of their traces has only one mobility mode: either human walking or car driving. The mobility mode mixed with walking, biking, and driving together in our selected traces is a more general scenario. In addition, some of their traces [23] are synthetic. However, our traces are raw data gathered from real applications, which inherently have noises. Hence, we still need to verify whether such traces are universally low rank.

We verify the low-rank property of the selected traces with the approach similar to Sect. 4.3.1. According to SVD, an $N \times T$ matrix X is decomposed as

$$X = U \Sigma V^T = \sum_{i=1}^{\min(n,m)} \sigma_i u_i v_i^T, \tag{6.3}$$

where U and V are two unitary matrices, V^T is the transpose of V, and $Sigma$ is an $N \times T$ diagonal matrix containing the singular value σ_i of X. Typically, the singular values σ_i are sorted as $\sigma_i \geq \sigma_i + 1, (i = 1, 2, \ldots, \min(N, T))$, where $\min(N, T)$ is the number of singular values. The rank of the matrix X, denoted by r, is the number of its nonzero singular values. The matrix is low rank if $r \ll \min(N, T)$. If the top-$\hat{r}$ singular values have a good approximation of the total singular values, i.e.,

$$\sum_{i=1}^{\hat{r}} \sigma_i \approx \sum_{i=1}^{\min(N,T)} \sigma_i, \tag{6.4}$$

this matrix is considered to be near low rank, and $\hat{r}$ is treated as its rank.

Fig. 6.3 Low-rank property in the investigated mobility traces

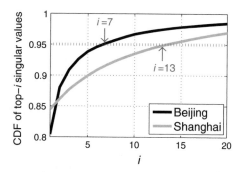

The CDF of the singular values obtained from the Beijing and Shanghai traces are shown in Fig. 6.3, where the x-axis presents the ith largest singular values, and the y-axis is the ratio between the sum of the top-i singular values and the sum of all singular values. We find that the total singular values are well approximated by only a few top singular values in both traces. For example, the top-7 σ_i of the Beijing and the top-13 σ_i of the Shanghai occupy more than 95% of their respective total values, while the total numbers of σ_is are 116 and 74, respectively. This observation reveals that both traces are of the near low-rank property. Hence, CS can be applied on them to achieve a promising recovery accuracy.

6.3.2 Overview

The proposed PPCS consists of three steps. First, users encrypt their sensed data and transmit the encrypted trajectories to the server. Note that the encrypted trajectories may not be complete because of the data missing issue. Second, the server performs CS on the collective data to recover the missing part of the encrypted trajectory for all users. Third, any individual user downloads the recovered and encrypted trajectory from the server, and decrypts it to obtain her original trajectory. An overview of these three steps is shown in Fig. 6.4. Briefly, the advantages of PPCS are:

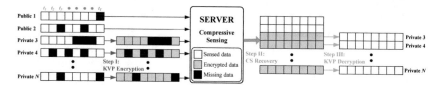

Fig. 6.4 PPCS oveview

- The design of PPCS is simple, and thus, it is easy to be implemented in practice.
- PPCS tactfully takes advantage of CS to provide significant privacy preservation strength while guaranteeing the accuracy of recovered trajectories.
- The high-complexity CS recovery is computed at the centralized server side. The distributed computing at the user side is the low-complexity encryption and decryption.
- The communication overhead of every user is very small.

6.3.3 Encrypt the Sensed Trajectories at Individual Users

The core component of PPCS is to encrypt the sensed trajectories at private users, so that only their encrypted trajectories are available at the server. Denote fen as the encryption operation. With a sensed trajectory $S(i)$ of the user i, the encrypted trajectory can be represented as

$$\mathbb{S}_i = f_{en}(S_i), \tag{6.5}$$

where S_i presents the i-th row vector in the matrix S.

In the next, we explain how the encryption operates in detail. In the system under consideration, public users are willing to share their trajectories, which are available at the server. At the first phase of encryption, a private user i randomly downloads K public vectors $D(1), D(2), \ldots, D(K)$ from all public vectors at the server, which is utilized to generate the encrypted vector $S(i)$. Only K-vector downloading does not lead to much communication overhead. In addition, random downloading brings more uncertainty for privacy preservation.

Then, user i generates a length-$(K + 1)$ random vector $< \psi_{i,0}, \psi_{i,1}, \psi_{i,2}, \ldots,$ $\psi_{i,K} >$ as her private key, which is not shared to any other including the server. Any key satisfies $\psi_{i,j} \in (0, 1)$ and $\sum_{j=0}^{\psi_{i,j}=1}$. With the public vectors and the private key, user i generates her encrypted vector $S(i)$ as

$$\mathbb{S}_i = (\psi_{i,0} S_i + \psi_{i,1} D_1 + \cdots + \psi_{i,K} D_K) \circ \Psi_i. \tag{6.6}$$

To demonstrate the encryption operation, let us consider the example shown in Fig. 6.5. Assume a private user $i = 4$ has downloaded $K = 2$ public vectors from the server (i.e., $D(1), D(2)$), and has generated the length-3 key $< \psi_{4,0}, \psi_{4,1}, \psi_{4,2} >$. The three vectors $S(4), D(1)$, and $D(2)$ are summed up with weight $\psi_{4,0}, \psi_{4,1}$, and $\psi_{4,2}$ respectively. For each null element in $S(4)$, the corresponding element in the resultant sum vector is treated as the missing data and the encrypted vector $S(4)$ is then transmitted to the server.

This encryption method is referred to as K-Vector Perturbation (KVP) in this chapter, because (1) from the aspect of matrix operation, fen is essentially a linear

Fig. 6.5 KVP encryption

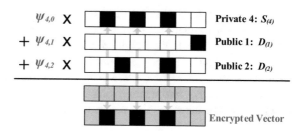

combination of K vectors in a matrix, and (2) the physical meaning of fen is to perturb the user trajectory with other K public trajectories.

Intuitively, the length of private key dominates the difficulty for adversaries to decrypting the original data. Hence, the value of K determines the privacy preservation strength offered by KVP. We will further discuss the impact of K on the performance of PPCS later.

6.3.4 Recover the Encrypted Trajectories at the Server

After collecting the encrypted trajectories from all private users and original trajectories of all public users, the server forms the encrypted matrix S of size $N \times T$. Then, crowdsensing recovery method applies CS on S and the completed encrypted trajectory matrix is obtained as $\hat{X} = f_{cs}(S)$.

The f_{cs} operation adopted in this chapter is the standard CS recovery. The procedures of f_{cs} are similar to those described in Sect. 4.3.2.

6.3.5 Decrypting the Recovered Trajectories at Individual Users

After the encrypted trajectories are recovered at the server, any individual user can download her corresponding encrypted trajectory and apply the decryption operation. Specifically, user i downloads $\hat{X}_i$ from the server, and locally decrypts it with the public vectors and her private key as

$$\hat{X}_i = (\hat{\mathbb{X}}_i - (\psi_{i,1}D_1 + \cdots + \psi_{i,K}D_K))/\psi_{i,0}, \tag{6.7}$$

where $\hat{(X)}_i$ is the approximation of X_i, i.e., the recovered complete trajectory of user i. Due to the local decryption and the private key, $\hat{X}_i$ is only known by user i herself. Then, a user can exploit map matching methods [27], which normally adjust the recovered trajectory by matching the nearest roads in the map, to further improve the accuracy.

At the end of this design, we discuss the impact of $\psi_{i,0}$. In PPCS, $\psi_{i,0}$ determines the weight of a original vector in the encrypted vector. On one hand, $\psi_{i,0}$ cannot be too small. When $\psi_{i,0} \to 0$, the weight of $X(i)$ in the encrypted $X(i)$ is too small, which will result in a poor recovery accuracy. On the other hand, $\psi_{i,0}$ cannot be too large. When $\psi_{i,0} \leftarrow 1$, $X(i) = X(i)$, which losses the effect of encryption. Empirically, we find that setting $\psi_{i,0}$ in the range $[0.2, 0.8]$ can guarantee a high recovery accuracy and privacy. The other weights still satisfy $\psi_{i,j|j\neq0} \in (0, 1)$ and $\sum_{j=0}^{K} \psi_{i,j} = 1$.

6.4 Theoretical Analysis

In this section, we analyze the performance of PPCS in three metrics: the trajectory recovery accuracy, the privacy preservation against eavesdroppers, and the privacy preservation against stalkers. Its complexity analysis is also presented.

6.4.1 Accuracy Analysis

Although recovering trajectory by CS has been shown to achieve a promising accuracy, we still need to make sure the KVP encryption operation does not degrade the accuracy.

We adopt the same metric in [23] to evaluate the recovery accuracy, namely, the recovery error ϵ. For user i, its recovery error ϵ_i is the geometric mean of the distance between the actual trajectory and the recovered trajectory, defined as

$$\epsilon_i = \frac{\|X_i - \hat{X}_i\|_2}{T}, \tag{6.8}$$

where $\|X_i - \hat{X}_i\|_2 = \sqrt{\sum_{j=1}^{T}(x_{ij} - \hat{x}_{ij})^2}$, and T is the total number of time slots along the trajectory.

With this accuracy metric, we have the following theorem stating that the KVP encryption operation does not degrade the recovery accuracy.

Theorem 6.1 *The proposed KVP is a homomorphic obfuscation method for CS. We define the homomorphic obfuscation property as follows. If a matrix X is near low rank, the recovery accuracy of a user i satisfies*

$$sup\|X_i - \hat{X}_i\|_2 = sup\|X_i - \tilde{X}_i\|_2, \tag{6.9}$$

where sup is the upper bound of $\|\cdot\|$, $\hat{X}$ is the trajectories recovered by CS with KVP (i.e., $\hat{X} = f_{de}(f_{cs}(f_{en}(X \circ \Phi))))$, $\tilde{X}$ is trajectories recovered by CS directly (i.e., $\tilde{X} = f_{cs}(X \circ \Phi)$), and $\hat{X}_i$ is the recovered by trajectory of user i.

Proof When a matrix is near low rank and the value of approximate rank is r, the value $\sum_{i=1}^{\min(N,T)} \sigma_i - \sum i = 1^r \sigma_i$ can be considered as noise [7], which is denoted as ξ. $\qquad\square$

According to existing work on the CS-based matrix completion [7, 14], we have the accuracy upper bound as

$$sup\|X - \widetilde{X}\|_2 = 4\sqrt{\frac{2\min(N,T)}{(1-\alpha}}\xi_1, \qquad (6.10)$$

where α is the data loss ratio in X, and ξ_1 is the noise of X.

Similarly, the accuracy upper bound of $\|\mathbb{X}\|_2$ can be represented as

$$sup\|\mathbb{X} - \hat{\mathbb{X}}\|_2 = 4\sqrt{\frac{2\min(N,T)}{(1-\alpha)}}\xi_2, \qquad (6.11)$$

where ξ_2 is the noise of $\mathbb{X}$.

From Fig. 6.5, we know that the KVP operation does not change the number of missing data. Consequently, the loss ratio α in Eq. 6.10 and in Eq. 6.11 has the same value. Combining Eqs. 6.10 and 6.11, we have

$$\frac{sup\|\mathbb{X} - \hat{\mathbb{X}}\|_2}{sup\|X - \widetilde{X}\|_2} = \frac{\xi_2}{\xi_1}. \qquad (6.12)$$

It is difficult to obtain the exact value of ξ_1 and ξ_2, which highly depends on the specific data. However, because KVP is a basic linear transformation, which can be presented as $\mathbb{X} = \Psi X$ and Ψ is the matrix of private keys ψ. Treating this transformation as a measurement operation in CS, we can obtain the noise ratio according to CS theory [7],

$$\frac{\xi_2}{\xi_1} = \frac{|\mu(\Phi, \Psi)|}{|\mu(\Phi, I)|}. \qquad (6.13)$$

Recall that Φ is the binary index matrix indicating the missing data. The coherence operation μ in Eq. 6.13 is defined as

$$\mu(\Phi, I) = \max_{1 \le i \ne j \le T} | < \Phi^{(i)}, I^{(j)} > |, \qquad (6.14)$$

where $\Phi^{(i)}$ is the i-th column vector of $\Phi_{N \times T}$, and $< \Phi^{(i)}, I^{(j)} >$ is the inner product of two vectors, i.e., $< \Phi^{(i)}, I^{(j)} >= (\Phi^{(i)})^T I^{(j)}$.

By the design of KVP, we have the Ψ matrix as follows, which is an example when $K = 2$ as shown in Fig. 6.5

$$\Psi = \begin{bmatrix} 1 & 0 & 0 & 0 & 0 \\ 0 & 1 & 0 & 0 & 0 \\ \psi_{3,1} & \psi_{3,2} & \psi_{3,0} & 0 & 0 \\ \vdots & \vdots & 0 & \ddots & 0 \\ \psi_{N,1} & \psi_{N,2} & 0 & 0 & \psi_{N,0} \end{bmatrix}. \tag{6.15}$$

Combine Eqs. 6.12, 6.13, 6.14, and 6.15, we can calculate the recovery error of user i as

$$\frac{sup\|X_i - \hat{X}_i\|_2}{sup\|X_i - \tilde{X}_i\|_2} = \frac{|\mu(\Phi, \Psi^{(i)})|}{|\mu(\Phi, I^{(i)})|} = \frac{\psi_{i,0}}{1}. \tag{6.16}$$

Because of the reasons that (1) the decryption operation $f_{de}(X(i)) = \hat{X}(i)$ is also a linear transformation according to Eq. 6.7; (2) all other variables such as Ds and ψs are known; and (3) since $\sum_{j=0}^{K} \psi_{i,j} = 1$, we know the error is linearly amplified according to weights

$$\frac{sup\|X_i - \tilde{X}_i\|_2}{sup\|X_i - \hat{X}_i\|_2} = \frac{\psi_{i,0} + \psi_{i,1} + \cdots + \psi_{i,p}}{\psi_{i,0}} = \frac{1}{\psi_{i,0}}. \tag{6.17}$$

Combining the above two equations, we have

$$sup\|X_i - \hat{X}_i\|_2 = sup\|X_i - \tilde{X}_i\|_2, \tag{6.18}$$

and the theorem is proved.

6.4.2 Privacy Preservation against Eavesdroppers

Privacy preservation is offered by PPCS. We discuss how PPCS protects privacy leakage against eavesdroppers (in this subsection) and stalkers (in the next subsection).

The location data are encrypted by individual users before transmitting them to the server. In this way, only encrypted data (the encrypted sensed trajectories sent from the users S, or the complete encrypted trajectories $\hat{X}$ recovered by CS) can be captured by eavesdroppers. These eavesdroppers can only infer the original user trajectory based on the exposed encrypted data $\hat{X}$. Therefore, we adopt the distortion δ defined in [34] to measure the similarity between the encrypted and the original data of every user

$$\delta_i = \frac{\sum_{j=1}^{T} |\hat{\mathbb{X}}_{i,j} - X_{(i,j)}|}{T}. \tag{6.19}$$

The value of δ presents the average per-location distortion between the encrypted and the original trajectories, and a larger δ indicates a stronger privacy preservation against eavesdroppers. In practice, the complete trajectory X is not always available due to the missing data issue. In this case, we adopt the recovered $\hat{X}$ to replace X in Eq. 6.19 for computing.

The PPCS scheme exploits KVP to obfuscate the user's personal trajectory. Since several trajectories are perturbed into one trajectory, even if an eavesdropper steals this combined trajectory, it is not easy to distinguish the original one. In the next, we derive the distribution of the distortion δ.

The encrypted vector is obtained via linearly combining K public vectors with weights ψs, and this encryption operation demonstrates significant randomness in that (1) the K public vectors are randomly selected from all public vectors and (2) the weight vector $< \psi_{i,0}, \psi_{i,1}, \ldots, \psi_{i,K} >$ is randomly generated. With these randomness, the original locations are mapped to other locations but still in the area of interests. As a result, we can use the random distance distribution to approximate the distortion of a given location and its encrypted data.

Consider a $w \times h$ rectangle area, the distortion distribution $\mathbb{P}(\delta \leq d)$ can be presented by a piecewise function [5]

$$
\mathbb{P}(\delta \leq d) = \begin{cases}
\dfrac{2}{w^2 h^2}(G(d) - G(0)) & d \in [0, h], \\[2mm]
\dfrac{2}{w^2 h^2}(G(h) - G(0)) & d \in (h, w], \\[2mm]
\dfrac{2}{w^2 h^2}(G(h) - G(\sqrt{d^2 - w^2})) \\[2mm]
\quad + F_h(\sqrt{d^2 - w^2}) & d \in (d, \eta],
\end{cases}
\tag{6.20}
$$

where

$$
G(z) = \int (h - z)\sqrt{d^2 - z^2}(2w - \sqrt{d^2 - z^2})dz,
\tag{6.21}
$$

$$
F_h(z) = 1 - (1 - z/h)^2, \text{ and } \eta = \sqrt{w^2 + h^2}.
\tag{6.22}
$$

With this distribution, the average distance between randomly selected points (i.e., the expectation of distortion $\bar{\delta}$) can be easily obtained.

To valid our analysis on the distortion distribution, we simulate in a rectangle area with $w = 4$ km and $h = 3$ km, and randomly generate a set of trajectories including a total number of 1×106 locations. Then we apply KVP on these trajectories and record the distances between the original locations and their corresponding encrypted locations. The statistic distribution of these distances is shown in Fig. 6.6, along with the probability distribution calculated according to Eq. 6.20. The average distance of these location pairs is also shown in the figure (i.e., $\bar{\delta} \approx 1.83$ km).

Two observations are obtained from these results. First, the distortion shows significant randomness over a large distance range. Second, the average distortion between the original and encrypted locations is relatively large compared to the area. These

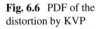

Fig. 6.6 PDF of the distortion by KVP

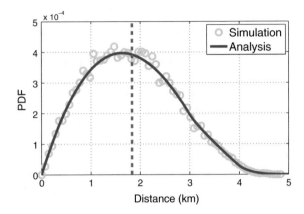

observations verify that there is no obvious pattern to infer the original locations through the encrypted locations.

6.4.3 Privacy Preservation Against Stalkers

Another adversary model is the stalker, who can obtain k actual location data of a user's trajectory. A stalker has two alternative methods to recover the trajectory: (1) Crack the private key based on the k data. (2) Run the crowdsensing recovery using these k data.

In the first method, to protect the user privacy, it is required that the trajectory $\hat{X}_i$ in Eq. (6.7) is unsolvable, even if the stalkers know the encrypted data $\hat{X}_i$, the decryption function f_{de}, and $k(k < K)$ actual location data of $X(i)$. The PPCS scheme resorts to the private keys against stalkers. From Eq. (6.7), we know

$$\hat{\mathbb{X}}_i = \psi_{i,0}\hat{X}_i + \psi_{i,1}D_1 + \cdots + \psi_{i,K}D_K. \tag{6.23}$$

It is possible for a stalker to obtain $\hat{X}_i$ by hacking the server, and she may also obtain the public vectors $D_i(i = 1, 2, \ldots, K)$. However, because the private keys $\psi_{i,j}(j = 0, 1, \ldots, K)$ are only known by the users themselves, a stalker resolving Eq. 6.23 needs the knowledge of at least $K + 1$ elements of X_i according to the theory of underdetermined system [9]. As a result, the stalker cannot resolve the original trajectory as long as the condition $k \leq K$ holds. As K is the control parameter adopted in PPCS, we can proactively adjust the number of public vectors used in the encryption operation according to the requirement of individual users.

In the second method, a stalk pretends herself as a private user and joins in the crowdsensing recovery. Many practical factors significantly affects the privacy-preserving such as the number of exposed location data k, the mobility model of users, the map structure, and etc. Some of these practical factors are not easy to be formulated. Hence, for this method, we conduct real trace-based simulations to verify the privacy preservation in practice (refer to Sect. 6.5.2).

6.4.4 Complexity Analysis

6.4.4.1 Computational Complexity

The KVP operation is locally run at user side. In KVP, $K + 1$ vectors with size $1 \times T$ need to be processed in encryption and decryption steps, which requires a computational complexity of $O((K + 1)T)$. This complexity costs negligible computing time owe to the capability of current GHz-level mobile devices.

At the server side, the main task is CS computing, which requires a computational complexity of $O(rNT\varrho)$ [23], where r is the rank of the to-be-recovered matrix and ϱ is the iteration numbers. Our evaluation experiences with Beijing and Shanghai traces reveal that $\varrho \leq 5$ in most cases. Since the server always has a strong computational capability, the CS operation is responsive in real-time.

6.4.4.2 Communication Overhead

In order to execute fen, a user should download K public vectors D_i from the server, and then upload a encrypted vector $\mathbb{S}_i$. Hence, the communication overhead is $O((K + 1)T)$. Moreover, in order to execute f_{de}, the user should download $\hat{\mathbb{X}}_i$, requiring another communication overhead of $O(T)$. As an example, with $K = 10$, $T = 500$ and a 16-bit operating system, the total amount of data exchange is about $(10 + 2)50016/8 = 12$ KB, which is a very light overhead for modern mobile applications.

6.4.5 Design Discussion

At the end of the analysis, we discuss the interesting design concern: *no public users*.

Public users are optional in PPCS. Even there is no public users, PPCS still works. To replace the roles of public vectors, the server can provide historical vectors (e.g., any trajectory with the same time interval yesterday), as long as the low-rank property is maintained. In addition, when a user has a high privacy requirement, she will demand a large K public vectors according to the analysis in Sect. 6.4. This inadequate K problem could also be solved by historical vectors.

6.5 Performance Evaluation

In this section, we evaluate the performance of PPCS in terms of both the data accuracy and the privacy.

6.5.1 Simulation Settings

We evaluate PPCS based on two real-world traces including walk, bike, and car data in Geolife [3], and taxi and bus data in SUVnet [2]. Using the same method in Sect. 6.3.1.1, we preprocess the raw data of Geolife and SUVnet by selecting complete trajectories as our ground truth to conduct our simulations. The selected traces are named Beijing traces with a size of 116 users $\times 355$ slots and Shanghai traces with a size of 74 users $\times 399$ slots, whose detailed descriptions are listed in Table 6.1.

In the trace-driven simulations, we randomly generate a $0 - 1$ matrix Φ with the same size as the original data trace. The element in Φ takes the value of 0 if its corresponding element in the data trace is missing and 1 otherwise. The ratio of the 0 elements to the total number of elements in Φ is controlled by the data loss ratio α, which is set to 0.5 by default unless otherwise specified. Then, we generate the sensed matrix S according to Eq. (6.6), i.e., $S = X \circ \Phi$. The proposed PPCS is applied on the sensed matrix S with K public vectors, and the recovered matrix $\hat{X}$ is obtained. Without loss of generality, the top-K rows in the original traces are treated as the public traces, and $K = 10$ by default. The reported results in the following are averaged over 100 simulation runs.

We adopt the CS-based crowdsensing recovery method introduced in Chap. 4 as a baseline, which is referred to as CS in the remaining of this section. With respect to the adversary model, we consider that an eavesdropper can steal all encrypted data $\hat{X}$. And the stalker has a part ($<10\%$) of real trajectory data.

6.5.2 Performance Analysis

6.5.2.1 Recovery Accuracy

We first evaluate the recovery accuracy with a default setting of $\alpha = 0.5$ and $K = 10$. The distributions of the recovery accuracies obtained by PPCS and CS with the two real-world traces are shown in Fig. 6.7. For example, Fig. 6.7a shows that the recovery errors of 50% users' trajectories are less than 10 m and the average recovery error is 53 m when applying PPCS on Beijing traces. Two observations are obtained from Fig. 6.7. First, the recovery accuracy obtained with PPCS and CS are comparable in both traces, which validates the correctness of the Theorem that PPCS can achieve

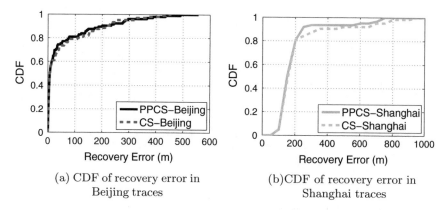

Fig. 6.7 Recovery accuracy comparison

similar recovery accuracy as the CS method. Second, the recovery errors are small. For instance, the recovery errors of 80% users with Beijing and Shanghai are less than 100 m and 200 m, respectively. These errors are tolerable in many cases because mechanisms such as map matching [12, 21, 27] can eliminate their impacts on the final recovered trajectories.

6.5.2.2 Privacy Against Eavesdroppers

Keeping $\alpha = 0.5$ and $K = 10$, next, we investigate the perturbation distortion obtained with PPCS. In Fig. 6.8a, we can see that the distortion between original and encrypted trajectories is enormous. For example, the distortion of 50% trajectories are over 4,000 m and the average distortion is more than 9,000 m with Beijing traces. Such distortion distances are quite large when compared with the road segment length in Beijing city. As a result, even if the encrypted trajectory is exposed to adversaries, the information leakage on the original trajectory is small, indicating a strong privacy preservation level. Another observation is that the distortion distribution shows no clear patterns. For example, the distortion distribution with Shanghai traces is nearly linear, but that with Beijing traces is more like a piecewise function. This patternless feature indicates that even the adversaries can obtain a large amount of the encrypted trajectories, the training methods based on this information would not facilitate them to infer the original trajectories.

As analysis in Sect. 6.4, PPCS needs a number of public (or historical) trajectories to perform the encryption. To investigate the impact of the amount of public trajectories on the distortion, we apply PPCS on the two traces with the number of public traces varying from 10 to 60 (the total number of users in Beijing and Shanghai are 116 and 74, respectively). The results in Fig. 6.8b demonstrate that there is no clear relation between the distortion and the number of available public traces. This observation alleviates our concern on whether the available number of public

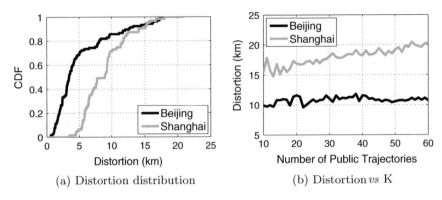

(a) Distortion distribution   (b) Distortion vs K

Fig. 6.8 Distortion versus eavesdroppers

trajectories will significantly degrade the distortion performance of PPCS. So the privacy-preserving level in PPCS is independent to the number of public vectors.

6.5.2.3   Privacy Against Stalkers

A stalker can treat the exposed k data of a user as a $(T - k)$ missing data trajectory and then utilizes PPCS to recover this trajectory. Next, we evaluate the privacy preservation offered by PPCS against stalkers, and the results are shown in Table 6.2. Recall that k is a small number in the stalker model. We set and evaluate the cases when 5 and 10% actual location data are captured by the stalks. In the case of 5%, the recovery error is more than 2,500 m with Shanghai traces and more than 400 m with Beijing traces. It is difficult to obtain the actual trajectory with such large errors. Even if a stalker has 10% actual trajectories, she cannot achieve a promising recovery accuracy. On the contrary, when the data loss ratio is $\alpha = 0.5$, the private users under PPCS has an excellent accuracy that always under 40 m with Beijing traces. In summary, our PPCS solution is able to effectively protect the privacy even when a few original data are exposed.

Table 6.2 Recovery error when stalkers have partial original data

Recovery error ϵ	Stalker (5%) (m)	Stalker (10%) (m)	User (50%) (m)
ϵ of Beijing	1409.36	366.47	38.99
ϵ of Shanghai	2510.48	1723.16	189.96

6.5.3 Illustrative Results

To demonstrate a clear view of the results obtained with PPCS, we show the recovered trajectory by PPCS/CS/Stalker and the encrypted trajectory against eavesdropper in Fig 6.9, using a 10-location original trajectory. All trajectories are fitted to roads by the map match method proposed in [29].

In Fig. 6.9a, the recovered trajectories by PPCS and CS are drawn when 4 locations along the trajectory are missing. We can see when 40% of original data are missing, PPCS still recovers the original trajectory with a high accuracy that is comparable to the result of CS. Moreover, Fig. 6.9a also shows the recovered trajectory of a stalker who applies PPCS with 3 stalked actual locations, which is a totally different trajectory compared with the original one.

The encrypted trajectory is shown in Fig. 6.9b. Comparing the latitude and the longitude in Fig. 6.9b with those in Fig. 6.9a, we find that the distortion between the encrypted trajectory and the original one is relatively large, indicating a strong defense against eavesdroppers. Furthermore, the encrypted results also form a sound trajectory in the map. This indicates that the eavesdroppers cannot easily determine whether the hacked trajectories are encrypted or not.

In addition, even an adversary can eavesdrop and stalk simultaneously, she can only obtain two separate results: "encrypted" as shown in Fig. 6.9b and "stalker" in 6.9a, but no further improvement on inferring the original trajectory.

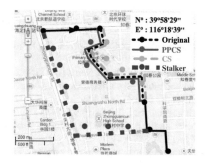
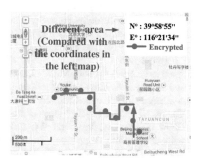

(a) The recovered trajectories by PPCS and CS are similar to the original one, but the trajectory recovered by a stalker is much different.

(b) The encrypted trajectory distorts the original one to a different area (refer to the latitude and the longitude) against eavesdroppers.

Fig. 6.9 Illustrative results of PPCS. (The dots are the PPCS/CS/Stalker/Encrypted results. The lines are the map matching results based on the dots.)

6.6 Summary

With the increasing popularity of location-based services, it is important to simultaneously consider the quality of service and user privacy. Focus on the trajectory recovery service, in this chapter, we saw an example of how homogeneous compressive sensing is applied in privacy preservation problem. We introduced a novel PPCS scheme, which uses compressive sensing to accurately recover the trajectories with the consideration of privacy. The core design of PPCS leverages the matrix transformation to include the privacy preservation into compressive sensing. Through extensive trace-based simulations, we demonstrate that PPCS not only effectively preserves the user privacy against eavesdroppers and stalkers, but also accomplishes comparable accuracy as the original CS design. Although we focus on the trajectory recovery in this work, the general PPCS can also be utilized in other privacy-preserving data recovery applications.

References

1. (2005) Trippermap service in flickr. http://www.flickr.com/services/apps/5121/
2. (2007) SUVnet data collected by Shanghai Jiao Tong University. http://wirelesslab.sjtu.edu.cn/download.html
3. (2009) Geolife data collected by microsoft research Asia. http://research.microsoft.com/en-us/projects/geolife/default.aspx
4. (2014) Facebook acquires company behind moves fitness app. http://www.theverge.com/2014/4/24/5647084/facebook-acquires-moves-fitness-app
5. Alagar VS (1976) The distribution of the distance between random points. J Appl Probab 13(3):558–566
6. Asuquo P, Cruickshank H, Morley J, Ogah CPA, Lei A, Hathal W, Bao S, Sun Z (2018) Security and privacy in location-based services for vehicular and mobile communications: an overview, challenges, and countermeasures. IEEE Internet Things J 5(6):4778–4802
7. Candes EJ, Plan Y (2010) Matrix completion with noise. Proc IEEE 98(6):925–936
8. Chow CY, Mokbel MF, Aref WG (2009) Casper*: query processing for location services without compromising privacy. Trans Database Syst (TODS) 34(4):24
9. Demmel JW, Higham NJ (1993) Improved error bounds for underdetermined system solvers. J Matrix Anal Appl 14(1):1–14
10. Ghinita G, Kalnis P, Khoshgozaran A, Shahabi C, Tan KL (2008) Private queries in location based services: anonymizers are not necessary. In: International conference on management of data (SIGMOD), ACM, pp 121–132
11. Ghose A, Li B, Liu S (2019) Mobile targeting using customer trajectory patterns. Manag Sci
12. Gong YJ, Chen E, Zhang X, Ni LM, Zhang J (2018) Antmapper: an ant colony-based map matching approach for trajectory-based applications. IEEE Trans Intell Transp Syst 19(2):390–401
13. Gruteser M, Grunwald D (2003) Anonymous usage of location-based services through spatial and temporal cloaking. In: International conference on mobile systems. ACM, Applications and Services (MobiSys), pp 31–42
14. Hegde C, Indyk P, Schmidt L (2014) Approximation-tolerant model-based compressive sensing. In: Proceedings of the twenty-fifth annual ACM-SIAM symposium on Discrete algorithms, Society for Industrial and Applied Mathematics, pp 1544–1561

15. Hoh B, Gruteser M (2005) Protecting location privacy through path confusion. In: Security and privacy for emerging areas in communications networks, IEEE, pp 194–205
16. Kido H, Yanagisawa Y, Satoh T (2005) An anonymous communication technique using dummies for location-based services. In: International conference on pervasive services (ICPS), IEEE, pp 88–97
17. Li XY, Jung T (2013) Search me if you can: privacy-preserving location query service. In: International conference on computer communications (INFOCOM), IEEE, pp 2760–2768
18. Liu J, Priyantha B, Hart T, Ramos HS, Loureiro AA, Wang Q (2012) Energy efficient gps sensing with cloud offloading. In: Conference on embedded network sensor systems (SenSys), ACM, pp 85–98
19. Liu S, Wang S, Jayarajah K, Misra A, Krishnan R (2013) Todmis: mining communities from trajectories. In: International conference on information & knowledge management (CIKM), ACM, pp 2109–2118
20. Ma CY, Yau DK, Yip NK, Rao NS (2013) Privacy vulnerability of published anonymous mobility traces. Trans Netw (TON) 21(3):720–733
21. Newson P, Krumm J (2009) Hidden markov map matching through noise and sparseness. In: International conference on advances in geographic information systems (SIGSPATIAL), ACM, pp 336–343
22. Quercia D, Leontiadis I, McNamara L, Mascolo C, Crowcroft J (2011) Spotme if you can: randomized responses for location obfuscation on mobile phones. In: International conference on distributed computing systems (ICDCS), IEEE, pp 363–372
23. Rallapalli S, Qiu L, Zhang Y, Chen YC (2010) Exploiting temporal stability and low-rank structure for localization in mobile networks. In: International conference on mobile computing and networking (MOBICOM), ACM, pp 161–172
24. Rosales R, Sclaroff S (1999) 3d trajectory recovery for tracking multiple objects and trajectory guided recognition of actions. In: Conference on computer vision and pattern recognition, IEEE, vol 2, pp 117–123
25. Scaglia G, Rosales A, Quintero L, Mut V, Agarwal R (2010) A linear-interpolation-based controller design for trajectory tracking of mobile robots. Control Eng Pract 18(3):318–329
26. Singh I, Butkiewicz M, Madhyastha HV, Krishnamurthy SV, Addepalli S (2013) Twitsper: tweeting privately. IEEE Secur Priv 11(3):46–50
27. Thiagarajan A, Ravindranath L, Balakrishnan H, Madden S, Girod L (2011) Accurate, low-energy trajectory mapping for mobile devices. USENIX
28. Wang J, Wang Y, Zhang D, Helal S (2018) Energy saving techniques in mobile crowd sensing: Current state and future opportunities. IEEE Commun Mag 56(5):164–169
29. White CE, Bernstein D, Kornhauser AL (2000) Some map matching algorithms for personal navigation assistants. Transp Res Part C: Emerg Technol 8(1):91–108
30. Wong WK, Cheung DWl, Kao B, Mamoulis N (2009) Secure knn computation on encrypted databases. In: International conference on management of data (SIGMOD), ACM, pp 139–152
31. Xia M, Gong L, Lyu Y, Qi Z, Liu X (2015) Effective real-time android application auditing. In: Symposium on security and privacy (SP), IEEE, pp 899–914
32. Xu T, Cai Y (2009) Feeling-based location privacy protection for location-based services. In: Conference on computer and communications security (CCS), ACM, pp 348–357
33. Zang H, Bolot J (2011) Anonymization of location data does not work: a large-scale measurement study. In: International conference on mobile computing and networking (MOBICOM), ACM, pp 145–156
34. Zhu J, Kim KH, Mohapatra P, Congdon P (2013) An adaptive privacy-preserving scheme for location tracking of a mobile user. Conference on sensor. Mesh and Ad Hoc Communications and Networks (SECON), IEEE, pp 140–148

Chapter 7
Converted Compressive Sensing for Multidimensional Data

Generally speaking, there are two types of data in mobile crowdsensing: (1) sensor data from the environment and, (2) user-provided information (e.g., a survey response). The data type we talked in the previous chapters all belong to the first type. This type of data typically has two dimensions, i.e., time dimension and location dimension (or user dimension in some cases). They can be easily stored in a matrix and most of them are low-rank, thus can be easily reconstructed via compressive sensing. However, the second type of data remains unmentioned. The user-provided information is not as canonical as sensor data, because in most cases, they are multidimensional. Hence, they are not naturally fitted in a matrix form and compressive sensing cannot be directly applied. In this chapter, we will focus on user-provided multidimensional data in mobile sensing and see how converted compressive sensing can be applied on such type of data to reduce the user burden. Unlike the previous chapters, instead of its two-dimensional extension, we will return to the original form of compressive sensing, and find the internal sparse properties of these multidimensional data, other than the two-dimensional low-rank property.

7.1 Background

Generally speaking, there are two major types of scenarios in mobile crowdsensing. In the first scenario, the information can be obtained directly by sensing devices. The obtained information is generally numeric values related to time and location (or user id). Thus, we call them two-dimensional data. The information collecting process need zero or little human interference. Location, temperature, noise and air quality all

This chapter is represented with permission from Proceedings of the 2015 ACM International Joint Conference on Pervasive and Ubiquitous Computing (pp. 659-670). ©2015 ACM, Inc. http://dx. doi.org/10.1145/2750858.2807523.

belong to this type of data. In the second scenario, the target phenomenon cannot be directly captured by sensors. The data is usually related to human. What is the health condition of people elder than 60? Are there rats in residential buildings? These are all examples of the second scenario. The data collected from these applications are generally more complicated and related to multiple dimensions (for example, the health condition of people may be related to its age, gender, occupation, stature, etc.)

No matter which scenario it belongs, all MCS applications are faced with common challenges: How to control the cost of data collection? How to deduce the data that is not actually collected? In the previous chapters, we applied compressive sensing to tackle these challenges for the MCS applications that belongs to the first scenario. However, for the second scenario, compressive sensing is not directly applicable. This is mainly due to the following reasons:

- *Compressive sensing is not applicable to multidimensional data*: As discussed in Chap. 3, the conventional compressive sensing is designed for one-dimensional vectors and other data types that can be easily vectorized. It is not trivial to vectorize the multidimensional data collected from MCS because there are too many ways to vectorize them we have no idea which way is appropriate and which way is unreasonable. Although the extension proposed in [9] make the compressive sensing directly applicable to two-dimensional matrices, compressive sensing is still not applicable to multidimensional data.
- *The sparsity properties in multidimensional data is unknown*: In the two-dimension-extended compressive sensing that is used from Chap. 4 to Chap. 8, *low-rank* is used as the sparsity property. However, in multidimensional data, low-rank property is no longer satisfied. An approach is needed to judge if the data is sparse and find the appropriate form of sparsity, so that the compressive sensing can be applied.

In this chapter, we will introduce a framework proposed in [8], which mainly focuses on multidimensional survey data, and the core contribution of this framework is an effective approach to apply compressive sensing to multidimensional data. In this chapter, we use the name of *converted compressive sensing* for the framework, but focus on how it handles the multidimensional data. Central to the framework is the *Data Structure Conversion* process and *Base learning* process. The *Data Structure Conversion* process is able to convert the raw data from multidimensional form into a form that is suitable for compressive sensing. The *Base learning* process helps find the latent sparse properties from the the converted data.

In the following sections, we will describe this framework in detail.

7.2   Problem Statement

In this section, we will first have a review of the basic conventional compressive sensing and briefly introduce the concept of base learning. Then, we will show an example to interpret what is multidimensional data collected from MCS survey.

7.2.1 Preliminary

In this chapter, the data we discussed is no longer low-rank matrix, so we will go back to conventional compressive sensing. In this part, we will briefly review the basics of compressive sensing that has been introduced in Chap. 3, and introduce the concept of base learning.

7.2.1.1 Sparse Property

Compressive sensing is a data sampling technique. A signal can be represented as a vector $\mathbf{y} \in \mathbb{R}^n$. It can be converted into another linear space under a certain base Ψ:

$$\mathbf{y} = \Psi \mathbf{x}, \tag{7.1}$$

where is the coordinate of $\mathbf{y}$ under the base Ψ. If the signal $\mathbf{y}$ is *sparse*, we can find a certain base Ψ so that most of the element in coordinate $\mathbf{x}$ is zero. If the number nonzero element in $\mathbf{x}$ is k and $k \ll n$, we say the signal $\mathbf{y}$ is k-sparse. The compressive sensing theory [6] allows us to accurately reconstruct the signal $\mathbf{y}$ from only m samples in it, where $m \ll n$ and $m \geq k \log n$.

In practice, it is difficult to find signals that are *strictly sparse*, i.e., most elements in $\mathbf{x}$ is exact 0. This is because noises always exist in the acquired signal. The sparse signal with noise is called *approximately sparse* signal, which means most elements in $\mathbf{x}$ is close to zero, instead of completely zero.

7.2.1.2 Sampling

The sampling process can be viewed as a linear transformation of the original signal $\mathbf{y}$. It can be mathematically represented as following:

$$\mathbf{z} = \Phi \mathbf{y} = \Phi \Psi \mathbf{x}, \tag{7.2}$$

where $\mathbf{z} \in \mathbb{R}^m$ is the sampled data and Φ is a linear encoder matrix of size $m \times n$. Suppose the original signal is $\mathbf{y} = [y_1, y_2, y_3, y_4, y_5, y_6]^T$, and only y_1, y_4 and y_5 are sampled, then the process can be represented as

$$\mathbf{z} = \Phi \mathbf{y} = \begin{bmatrix} 1 & 0 & 0 & 0 & 0 & 0 \\ 0 & 0 & 0 & 1 & 0 & 0 \\ 0 & 0 & 0 & 0 & 1 & 0 \end{bmatrix} \times \begin{bmatrix} y_1 \\ y_2 \\ y_3 \\ y_4 \\ y_5 \\ y_6 \end{bmatrix} = \begin{bmatrix} y_1 \\ y_4 \\ y_5 \end{bmatrix}. \tag{7.3}$$

7.2.1.3 Data Reconstruction

The data reconstruction in compressive sensing is the process that deduce the original signal $y \in \mathbb{R}^n$ that is k-sparse under the base Ψ from the sampled signal $z \in \mathbb{R}^m$. Because $y = \Psi x$, finding y is equivalent to finding x which has at most k nonzero elements. Ideally, l_0-norm minimization should be used to find appropriate x. This is equivalent to finding an x with the smallest l_0-norm:

$$\text{Objective: } \min \|\hat{x}\|_0$$
$$\text{Subject to: } z = \Phi\Psi\hat{x}, \tag{7.4}$$

where $\|x\|_0$ is the l_0 norm of x, which indicates the number of nonzero elements in x. However, this is not applicable in practice. This is because the optimization problem (7.4) is NP-hard and cannot be solved with a reasonable time complexity. Thus, the problem is transformed into many other forms. We will introduce a commonly used solution in Sect. 7.3.5.

7.2.1.4 The Concept of Base Learning

Here the base Ψ plays a critical role in finding the sparse property hidden in the original signal. In practice, some standard bases such as Discrete Cosine Transform (DCT) base or Fourier base work well for some specific type of signals. However, These standard bases are not suitable to all kinds of data. The data discussed in this chapter is one of these types of data. The data is indeed sparse, but the form of sparse is unknown. To find the hidden base Ψ, we can train the base through historical data. This is the core idea of *base learning*.

Given a set of historical data $Y = \{y_1, y_2, \ldots, y_N\}$ and a predefined sparsity level k, *base learning* aims to find a appropriate base Ψ the corresponding coordinate x_i that minimize the total error between the given historical data and its sparse representation:

$$\text{Objective: } \min \sum_{i=1}^{N} \|y_i - x_i\|_2$$
$$\text{Subject to: } \|x_i\|_0 \leq k, \tag{7.5}$$

where $\|x\|_2 = \sqrt{\sum_{j=1}^{n} x_j}$ is the l_2 norm of the vector x, and $\|x\|_0$ is the l_0 norm of x, which indicates the number of nonzero elements in x.

7.2.2 Multidimensional Data Problem

Table 7.1 shows an example of a set of multidimensional crowdsensing data. The crowdsensing application aims to survey how many businesses within different

Table 7.1 Multidimensional survey data

Year	County	Industry	Frequency
2011	Queens, NY	Real Estate	16143
2010	Dallas, TX	Shoe Store	61
2010	Dallas, TX	Real Estate	18089
2011	Queens, NY	Shoe Store	78
...	...	...	...

industries fit into the business statistics category of being *non-employers*—in other words, they do not have any paid staff besides the business owners.

The raw data consists of four columns: year of the census, county where the employers located in, industries the employers belong to, and the number of the *non-employers*. The last column (the frequency of the *non-employers*) is the target data that we wanted, and the other three columns are three dimensions that the target data is related to.

It is not a good idea to treat the target data as a single vector. This is because the data are essentially related to different dimensions, and we do not know the impact of each dimension. Thus, we cannot guarantee the sparse property of the data.

In the next section, we will see how the raw multidimensional data is processed through *Data Structure Conversion*, and how compressive sensing is applied to the processed data.

7.3 Converted Compressive Sensing

In this section, we will describe the *converted compressive sensing* framework proposed in [8], which makes it possible to apply compressive sensing to user-provided multidimensional information.

7.3.1 Overview

The top-level design of *converted compressive sensing* is shown in Fig. 7.1. It is comprised of two parts: *Offline* part and *Online* part. In the offline part, the historical data is used to generate the pattern for *Data Structure Conversion*, and then convert the format of the raw data. Then, the converted data is used as the training set for base learning. The output of the offline part is twofold. The first one is a base Ψ for the reconstruction in compressive sensing. Moreover, the pattern for data structure conversion is also deduced from the historical data in an offline manner.

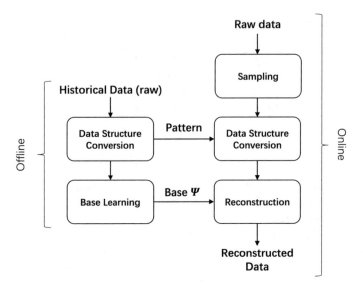

Fig. 7.1 Flow chart of converted compressive sensing

Table 7.2 Converted data

	Queens, NY 2011	Dallas, TX 2010	...
Real Estate	16143	18089	...
Shoe Store	78	61	...
...	...	...	...

The online part of *CCS* is the data reconstruction process. First, the raw data is sampled so that we get a subset of the original data. Then, the format of raw data is converted according to the pattern generated in the offline part. Finally, the converted data is reconstructed via a specific compressive sensing reconstruction algorithm.

There are four critical components in the *converted compressive sensing* framework:

- *Data Structure Conversion*: This is the critical step of *converted compressive sensing*, which enables us to apply CS techniques to multidimensional data. The converted data is in a matrix manner. Table 7.1 shows an example of the converted data corresponding to the *non-employers* data shown in Table 7.1. The pattern of the pattern of *Data Structure Conversion* is a critical factor to the sparsity level of data and the performance of data reconstruction. The *pattern-generating* procedure is conducted offline, prior to data collection.
- *Base Learning*: Given the converted matrix form, as shown in Table 7.2, an existing base learning algorithm is used to train a set of potential bases in an offline manner. Note, because of the complex structure typically existing in survey data the most commonly used bases, such as a DCT base, do not work well.

- *Sampling*: The sampling step is just an abstraction of data reduction. It can be either *active* (The sampling method is deliberately designed to reduce the size of the needed data. The scenario discussed in Chap. 8 is an example) or *passive* (Some part of the data is not available for some non-artificial reasons, e.g., the data is missed, as the scenario discussed from Chap. 4 to Chap. 6)
- *Reconstruction*: After collecting the sampled data set, we conduct a compressive sensing reconstruction algorithm to recover the original data, e.g., the number of non-employer businesses in every industry field shown in Table 7.1. This step is conducted online, i.e., every time the data is collected from users.

In the rest of this section, we will describe these components one by one.

7.3.2 Data Structure Conversion

Generally speaking, the *Data Structure Conversion* phase can be also divided into two parts: *conversion pattern generatiom (offline)* and *data aggregation (online)*.

7.3.2.1 Conversion Pattern Generation

In the collected multidimensional data, there is always a column called *target data*, as the column *Frequency* in the example data shown in Table 7.1. This column is the subject of our algorithm, while the other columns (dimensions) are just descriptors of the *target data*. The core idea of *data structure conversion* is to classify the dimensions according to their correlation with the *target data*. Some dimensions are closely related to the *target data*. For example, in Table 7.1, the *Industry* is most likely to have great impact on the *target data*—the *Number of non-employees*, while the other two dimensions does not show much relation to the *target data*. The *conversion pattern generation* procedure starts from the calculation of correlations.

By exploring the correlations between dimensions and *target data*, the dimensions can be classified into two categories: *sampling group* and *training group*. The *sampling group* dimensions are expected to present the inherent correlations with the target column, so that the data organized according to the *sampling group* can form a signal vector **y**, in which the elements have strong correlations, and thus is *(approximately) sparse*. On the other hand, the *training group* should be only loosely correlated to the target column. Different vectors across training groups should not be strongly correlated so that the vectors in the training set during base learning are independent.

The detailed process of *conversion pattern generation* is shown in Algorithm 7.1. First, from line 1 to line 3, the correlations between candidate columns are calculated and stored in a correlation matrix $C = [c(i, j)]_{d \times d}$, where d is the number of column in the raw data (including *target data*). Here, linear correlation is used due to its simplicity and feasibility. From line 7 to line 17, each columns in the raw data is

---

Algorithm 7.1: Conversion pattern generation

Input : Raw multidimensional data $R = \{col_1, col_2, \ldots, col_d\}$; The *target* column tar;
             Predefined threshold c_{tar}, c_{can}

Output: *sampling* group $\mathbb{S}$ and *training* group $\mathbb{T}$

1 **for** $i \leftarrow 1$ *to* d **do**
2   **for** $j \leftarrow 1$ *to* d **do**
3        $C(i, j) \leftarrow$ correlation between col_i and col_j;

4 $\mathbb{C} \leftarrow$ column indices of R, except for tar;
5 $\mathbb{S} \leftarrow \emptyset$;
6 $\mathbb{T} \leftarrow \emptyset$;
7 **while** $\mathbb{C}$ *is not empty* **do**
8     $k_0 \leftarrow \arg\max_{k_0} |C(k_0, tar)|(k_0 \in \mathbb{C})$;
9   **if** $|C(k_0, tar)| \geq c_{tar}$ **then**
10   add k_0 into $\mathbb{S}$;
11   remove k_0 from $\mathbb{C}$;
12   **foreach** k_1 *in* $\mathbb{C}$ **do**
13   **if** $|C(k_1, tar)| \geq c_{can}$ **then**
14   add k_1 into $\mathbb{S}$; remove k_1 from $\mathbb{C}$;

15   **else**
16   add k_0 into $\mathbb{T}$;
17   remove k_0 from $\mathbb{C}$;

18 **return** $\mathbb{S}$ *and* $\mathbb{T}$;

---

traversed and classified into *sampling group* or *training group*. Columns with high correlation with *target* is put in the *sampling group* while the columns with low correlation to the *training group*. Specifically, c_{tar} is a predefined threshold to judge whether a column should be classified as *sampling group*.

It is worth noting that from line 12 to line 14, we also classify the column that is relevant (judged by the predefined threshold c_{can}) to the selected k_0 as the sampling group. This is designed to reduce the number of missing values in the final data matrix produced by this algorithm. The procedure guarantees that the columns in the training group are relatively independent to the columns in sampling group.

The threshold c_{tar} and c_{can} are determined via experiment on the historical data. They can also be manually fine-tuned to ensure sufficient amounts of data are in both the *sampling* and *training groups*, in order to make the *base learning* and *reconstruction* steps more efficient.

7.3.2.2 Data Aggregation

Data aggregation is the process apply the *conversion pattern* (i.e., *sampling groups and training groups*) to raw data, and transform the raw data into matrix form. This process is done in an online manner. Specifically, consider a group of *sampling columns* $\mathbb{S} = [S_1, S_2, \ldots, S_s]$ and *training columns* $\mathbb{T} = [T_1, T_2, \ldots, T_t]$, in which each column S_i and T_i is comprised of $|S_i|$ and $|T_i|$ different elements, respectively. The mixed *sampling dimension* and *training dimension* should be $\mathbb{D}_S = [S_1 \times S_2 \times \cdots \times S_s]$ and $\mathbb{D}_T = [T_1 \times T_2 \times \cdots T_t]$, respectively, where $\times$ is the Cartesian product.

Take the *non-employer* survey data as an example, the field of industry is used to form the sampling groups because of its high correlation with the target while the other two columns are used to form *training dimension*. The industry field has two elements: $[Real Estate, Shoe Store]$ so the *sampling dimension* is comprised of $[Real Estate, Shoe Store]$. Similarly, The two *training columns* are comprised of $[2010, 2011]$ and $[Queens NY, Dallas TX]$, respectively. In principle, the training dimension should contain $2 \times 2 = 4$ elements. However, because the combination $(2010, Queens NY)$ and $(2011, Dallas TX)$ is empty, the final result of training dimension contains only two elements $[(2011, Queens NY), (2010, Dallas TX)]$. The size of real-world data set will be much larger than this. For example, later during the evaluation, the aggregated matrix is comprised of 3140(counties)$\times 5$(years), resulting in 15700 column of vectors of the length of 475(industries).

7.3.3 Base Learning

Base learning is able to uncover the correlation (i.e., *sparse property*) within *sampling group* vectors, and find a best basis Ψ to represent it. Due to the various properties of different survey data, the standard bases such as DCT of Fourier bases that are widely applied to natural signals (e.g., temperature, noise, etc.) are no longer suitable. Next, a *base learning process* is introduced to discover a suitable base.

7.3.3.1 K-SVD Algorithm

Theoretically, the optimal base can be found by solving the optimization problem in Eq. 7.6, i.e., find the base under which the historical data has the best sparse representations. However, this is not feasible because the problem is non-convex and computationally hard to solve. *K-SVD* is an alternative scheme to solve this problem.

$$\text{Objective: } \min \sum_{i=1}^{N} \|\mathbf{y_i} - \mathbf{x_i}\|_2$$
$$\text{Subject to: } \|\mathbf{x_i}\|_0 \leq k, \tag{7.6}$$

In essential, *K-SVD* is an iterative algorithm that alternately update the coordinates $\mathbf{x_i}$s and the base Ψ. Specifically, *K-SVD* first initialize the base Ψ, and then iteratively conduct the following procedure until convergence:

1. Fix Ψ and compute the best $\mathbf{x_i}$s by solving the following problem:

$$\text{Objective: } \min \|\mathbf{y_i} - \Psi \mathbf{x_i}\|_2$$
$$\text{Subject to: } \|\mathbf{x_i}\|_0 \leq k. \tag{7.7}$$

This problem is also the basic form of compressive sensing reconstruction. The solve of this problem will be introduced in Sect. 7.3.5

2. Fix x_is and update the Ψ column by column. The readers can refer to [5] for the detailed steps to update Ψ.

7.3.3.2   Multiple Base Learning

Theoretically, we do not know the sparse level k in advance. In practice, k is usually calculated from the sampling rate m according to the inequality

$$m \geq k \log n, \tag{7.8}$$

which is proved by compressive sensing theory [6]. Because the sampling rate is not a fixed value, we need to change the value of k when m changes. As a result, multiple bases is trained for different value of k. In *converted compressive sensing*, bases for different value of k are trained separately in an offline manner and stored in a dictionary. During the reconstruction phase, first, the optimal k is calculated from the sampling rate m, and the corresponding k is looked up from the dictionary.

7.3.4   Sampling in Converted Compressive Sensing

Data sampling can be either active or passive. In active sampling, the organizer deliberately discard part of the signal to compress the signal size. Compressive Crowd-sensing discussed in Chap. 8 is an example of active sampling, although it is not random sampling. In passive sampling, the sampling procedure is not controlled by human. Instead, the data is simply *lost*, due to various reasons. The cases discussed from Chap. 4 to Chap. 6 all belong to this category. In this chapter, we do not care whether the sampling is active or passive.

7.3.5   Reconstruction in Converted Compressive Sensing

Given the sampled data, we first aggregate them into a matrix representation, according to the grouping columns decided by *data structure conversion pattern generation*. Each column in this matrix is a vector that can be projected into the trained base Ψ to recover a *sparse representation* (i.e., x in Eq. 7.2) of the target. Then, the missing (unsampled) target values can be recovered by simply multiplying the base with the recovered *sparse representation*:

$$\hat{y} = \Psi \hat{x}. \tag{7.9}$$

Algorithm 7.2: Orthogonal Matching Pursuit

Input : Dictionary $\mathbf{D} = [\mathbf{d_1}, \mathbf{d_2}, \ldots, \mathbf{d_n}]$; Sampled signal $\mathbf{z} \in \mathbb{R}^m$; Sparse level k
Output: Sparse representation $\hat{\mathbf{x}} \in \mathbb{R}^n$

1 $\mathbf{r_0} \leftarrow \mathbf{z}$;   /* Initial the residual vector */
2 $\Lambda \leftarrow \emptyset$;   /* Indices of the nonzero elements in $\hat{\mathbf{x}}$ */
3 $\mathbf{D_0} \leftarrow \emptyset$;   /* Selected columns in $\mathbf{D}$ */
4 **for** $t \leftarrow 1$ *to* k **do**
5      $\lambda_t \leftarrow \arg\max_{j \notin \Lambda} | < \mathbf{r_{t-1}}, \mathbf{d_j} > |$;
6   put λ_t into Λ;
7      $\mathbf{D}_t \leftarrow [\mathbf{D}_{t-1}, \mathbf{d}_{\lambda_t}]$;
8      $\mathbf{x}_t \leftarrow \arg\max_{\mathbf{x}} \|\mathbf{z} - \mathbf{D}_t\mathbf{x}\|_2$;
9      $\mathbf{r}_t \leftarrow \mathbf{z} - \mathbf{D}_t\mathbf{x}_t$;
10 $\hat{\mathbf{x}} \leftarrow zeros(1, n)$;
11 **for** $i \leftarrow 1$ *to* k **do**
12     $\hat{\mathbf{x}}[\Lambda[i]] \leftarrow \mathbf{x_m}[i]$;
13 **return** $\hat{\mathbf{x}}$;

Now the problem is, given the sampled data $\mathbf{z}$, sample matrix Φ and the trained base Ψ, how to recover the *sparse representation* $\hat{\mathbf{x}}$? In *converted compressive sensing*, *Orthogonal Matching Pursuit (OMP)* algorithm proposed in [7] is adopted. Suppose the length of $\mathbf{y}$ is n, the *sparse level* is k, the *sampling rate* is m, *OMP* uses a greedy approach to solve the following l_2-norm optimization problem:

$$\begin{aligned} \text{Objective: } & \arg\min_{\hat{\mathbf{x}}} \|\mathbf{z} - \mathbf{D}\hat{\mathbf{x}}\|_2 \\ \text{Subject to: } & \|\hat{\mathbf{x}}\|_0 \leq k, \end{aligned} \tag{7.10}$$

where $\mathbf{D} = \Phi\Psi$ is an $m \times n$ matrix called the *dictionary matrix*.

The procedure of *OMP* is shown in Algorithm 7.2. The core idea of *OMP* is as following: If the ith element in $\mathbf{x}$ is *zero*, then the ith column in the *dictionary matrix* will have no impact when calculating $\mathbf{z} = \mathbf{Dx}$. Thus, *OMP* attempt to select the top-k columns in the *dictionary matrix* $\mathbf{D}$ that contribute most in minimizing $\|\mathbf{z} - \mathbf{D}\hat{\mathbf{x}}\|_2$ (Line 4 to Line 9), and setting the corresponding element in $\hat{\mathbf{x}}$ as nonzero (Line 12). The readers can refer to [7] for more interpretation and proving of the *OMP* algorithm.

7.4 Evaluation

In this section, we will briefly review the performance evaluation of the *converted compressive sensing* framework. Again, we just concentrate on the key points of the evaluation. The reader can refer to [8] for more detailed results and analysis.

7.4.1   Experiment Setup

7.4.1.1   Data set

A group of real-world data sets are used in the evaluation, namely, rat infestation reports [2], noise complaints [1], non-employer statistics [4], and housing attribute reports [3]. These data sets have a variety of dimensions ranging from 2 to 43. The readers can refer to [8] for more information of the size, format an preprocess of these data.

Active random sampling are performed to all these data sets in the experiments. This means that the underlying data set are selected based on randomly selected values of the sampling group of columns (e.g., selecting samples that belong to a randomly selected set of industries in the non-employer data set).

7.4.1.2   Evaluation Metric

In the evaluation, each vector grouped by the *sampling group* is considered as an entry. The data in a entry is judged as *accurate* if $|\hat{s} - s|/|s| < \tau$, where s and $\hat{s}$ are the original data and reconstructed data in the entry, respectively, and τ is a predefined threshold. The performance of reconstruction algorithm is judged as the percentage of accurate entries, i.e.,

$$Acc = \frac{\#Acuurate\,Entries}{\#All\,Entries}. \tag{7.11}$$

7.4.1.3   Comparison Baselines

Four baselines are used as baselines, namely,

- *Conventional CS*: This approach is similar to *converted compressive sensing*, while it does not perform base learning, and use a standard Fourier base instead.
- *Linear Interpolation*: A method of curve fitting using linear polynomials.
- *Spline Interpolation*: A method of curve fitting using piecewise cubic splines.
- *Kriging Interpolation*: A geographical interpolation method. In the evaluation, this method is only used in the data set with clear spatial components.

Moreover, an additional *Sampling Only* method is used as a lower bound for the performance. In this method, no reconstruction algorithm is used.

7.4.2 Performance of Base Training

In previous sections, it is proclaimed that the commonly used standard bases such as Fourier base and DCT base do not fit the multidimensional data in this chapter, and thus adopted *base learning* method to discover the optimal base. In this part, you can see why base learning is necessary. Figure 7.2 shows the distribution of coefficient under Fourier base and the trained base. We can observe from Fig. 7.2b that under Fourier base, there are lots of large coefficients distributed all over the coordinate vector **x**. In contrast, after base learning, only a couple of coefficients have large value, while the other coefficients are close to *zero*. This means that compared with the standard Fourier base, the trained base can represent the sparse property in the data set much more efficiently.

On the other hand, we can also observe from Fig. 7.2a that in rat infestation reports data set, lots of coefficients still remain large even under the trained base. This may be because that the rat infestation reports data set itself is not sparse. This also shows a limitation of the *converted compressive sensing* framework: if the data set does not have intrinsic sparse property, the *converted compressive sensing* will not perform well.

7.4.3 Performance of Data Reconstruction

The performance of data reconstruction on different data set is shown in Fig. 7.3. On both four data sets, the *converted compressive sensing* (Converted CS) outperforms

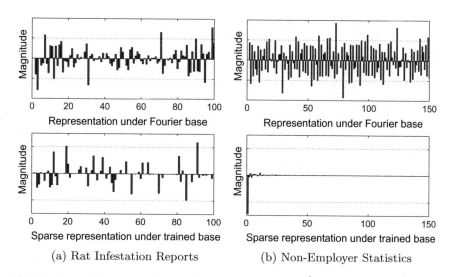

(a) Rat Infestation Reports (b) Non-Employer Statistics

Fig. 7.2 Comparison of different bases

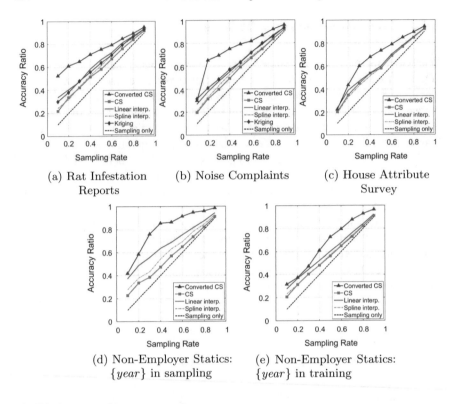

(a) Rat Infestation   (b) Noise Complaints   (c) House Attribute
      Reports   Survey

(d) Non-Employer Statics: (e) Non-Employer Statics:
    {*year*} in sampling   {*year*} in training

Fig. 7.3 Accuracy of data reconstruction

the other baseline methods. Specifically, the difference between Fig. 7.3d, e shows
the influence of *data structure conversion*. Recall that in *non-employer* survey data
set, there are three columns that are related to the *target*: *industry, year, and county*.
Figure 7.4 shows that the correlation between *industry* and *target* is large, while the
county does not show much correlation with *target*. Consequently, *industry* is classified as *sampling column* while *county* as *training group*. The correlation between
year and *target* is higher than that of *county* and lower than that of *industry*. *Year* is
classified in *sampling group* in Fig. 7.3d and *training group* in Fig. 7.3e. It can be
clearly seen that when *year* is in *sampling group*, the accuracy ratio of data reconstruction is much higher than classifying *year* in *training group*.

7.5   Summary

In this chapter, we focused on user-provided information in mobile crowdsensing. Unlike the data discussed in the previous chapters, user-provided information
describes complicated phenomenons and is typically multidimensional. This hinders

Fig. 7.4 Correlation between columns and *target*

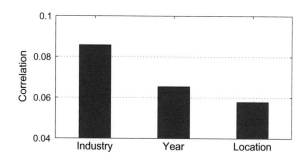

the direct application of compressive sensing. To address this problem, we introduced a converted compressive sensing framework proposed in [8], which is able to convert the data structure of the original data into a form that is suitable for compressive sensing. Moreover, the *converted compressive sensing* also conducts *base training* on the historical data in order to accurately capture the sparse property of specific type of data. Finally, *CCS* adopts *Orthogonal Matching Pursuit* which is proposed in [7] to solve the compressive sensing problem.

References

1. (2014) Noise complaints heatmap-nyc open data. https://data.cityofnewyork.us/social-services/noisecomplaints-heatmap/654p-getv
2. (2014) Rat sighting reports-nyc open data. https://data.cityofnewyork.us/social-services/ratsightings/3q43-55fe
3. (2017) Characteristics of new housing—united states census bureau. https://www.census.gov/construction/chars/
4. (2017) Non-employment statistics—united states census bureau. http://www.census.gov/econ/nonemployer/
5. Aharon M, Elad M, Bruckstein A et al (2006) K-svd: an algorithm for designing overcomplete dictionaries for sparse representation. Trans Signal Process 54(11):4311
6. Donoho DL (2006) Compressed sensing. Trans Inf Theory (TIT) 52(4):1289–1306
7. Tropp JA, Gilbert AC (2007) Signal recovery from random measurements via orthogonal matching pursuit. Trans Inf Theory (TIT) 53(12):4655–4666
8. Xu L, Hao X, Lane ND, Liu X, Moscibroda T (2015) More with less: lowering user burden in mobile crowdsourcing through compressive sensing. In: International joint conference on pervasive and ubiquitous computing (Ubicomp), ACM, pp 659–670
9. Zhang Y, Roughan M, Willinger W, Qiu L (2009) Spatio-temporal compressive sensing and internet traffic matrices. ACM SIGCOMM Comput Commun Rev ACM 39:267–278

Chapter 8
Compressive Crowdsensing for Task Allocation

In the previous chapters, we focus on what compressive sensing can do AFTER the data is collected. In chapter one, we will see what compressive sensing can do BEFORE the data is collected or DURING the data collection process. Most crowdsensing applications require data from large area, e.g., downtown area of a large city. In general, it is neither economical nor necessary to collect data from all the target area during all the data collection period. Instead, we need only select a subset of the target area as sample, and deduce value of the remaining unsensed data. This is the basic idea of Compressive Crowdsensing (CCS). There are two major problems in CCS: 1. How many locations and which locations should be selected as sample? 2. How to deduce the unsensed data accurately? The second problem can be solved via the method introduced in Chap. 3, while the first problem has not been mentioned in this book. The first problem is basically a form of task allocation problem. In this chapter, we will have a close look at CCS and use compressive sensing to solve its task allocation problem.

8.1 Background

Data quality and *cost* are two primary concerns of MCS organizers, especially when the sensing area is large. On one hand, MCS applications require high-quality data that can well represent the value of the data from the target area, which usually means collecting as much data as possible. On the other hand, more collected data means more participants and more costs to recruit them. The MCS organizers also want to minimize the cost. This brings about a trade-off between data quality and cost.

This chapter is represented with permission from Proceedings of the 2015 ACM International Joint Conference on Pervasive and Ubiquitous Computing, pp. 683–694. ©2015 ACM, Inc. http://dx.doi.org/10.1145/2750858.2807513.

© Springer Nature Singapore Pte Ltd. 2019
L. Kong et al., *When Compressive Sensing Meets Mobile Crowdsensing*, https://doi.org/10.1007/978-981-13-7776-1_8

In location-centric MCS applications, the target area is usually divided into sub-areas, or *cells*. The value in each cells is considered as the same. To address the data quality concern, *coverage ratio* is often used as a major metric. There are two types of coverage ratio: *full coverage* (the coverage of all sensing cells) [12, 14] and *probabilistic ratio* (the coverage of most sensing cells) [2, 6, 9, 11, 15]. By ensuring high coverage ratio, the MCS organizers are able to obtain the representative data for the target area, and further construct a full sensing picture. In essence, the data quality requirement is to *obtain a reasonably accurate sensing value for each cell, either through direct sensing or deduction.*

In order to achieve high coverage ratio, the most direct approach is to recruit participants and collect data from all the cells. Although high-quality data is more likely to obtain, this approach does not take the economic factor into consideration. When the target area is large (e.g., the urban area of a big city), the cost of recruiting participants for all the cells in the area is unaffordable. To tackle this problem, a possible solution is to optimize incentive mechanism and reduce incentive budget for participants. However, the overall cost can still be significant because too many participants are required.

In order to further reduce the number of needed participants, a new concept, Compressive Crowdsensing (CCS), is proposed. In CCS, only a small portion of cells is sensed, while a certain requirement of overall data accuracy is also satisfied. This is possible because in most cases, there are strong intrinsic temporal and spatial relationships between data from different cells, and thus theoretically, the data from unsensed cells can be reconstructed.

With the insight of CCS in mind, instead of coverage ratio, the *overall sensing accuracy* is used as the data quality metric. The usage of this metric tries to minimize the number of required participants by actively selecting a minimal number of cells for task allocation and deduce the missing data of unsensed cells by further exploit the temporal and spatial correlations, on the premise that the overall data accuracy meets a predefined bound.

The basic idea can be illustrated by the following use case. In the use case, the target area is the urban area of a city, which is divided into cells. An MCS organizer launches an environment temperature monitoring task in this area. The requirements of the task are as following:

- The full temperature sensing map needs to be updated once every hour (sensing cycle).
- In each sensing cycle, the mean absolute error for the whole area should be less than 0.25 (predefined bound).

In each sensing cycle, to meet the data quality requirement while minimizing the number of the allocated tasks, the organizer actively selects a subset of the cells to sense physically, i.e., allocating tasks to the participants in those selected cells. Based on the sensed temperature values of those selected cells, the temperature values of the remaining cells are deduced.

There are two major challenges in the above use case:

(1) *How many and which cells should be chosen for task allocation?* In each cycle, the organizer needs to select a minimal combination of cells that can represent for the whole target area. To address this problem, the concept of *salient cells* is proposed, which is defined as the cell whose sensing values can help deduce the values of other cells to the maximum extent. Now the problem become: How to identify *salient cells*. This is not trivial in an online manner. Without knowing the real value of the data in a cell, it is hard to know how much this value can influence the deduced value of other cells.

(2) *How to quantitatively estimate the data quality online without knowing the values of unsensed cells?* In each sensing cycle, the real value of the unsensed cells are unknown, thus it is impossible to compare the deduced value with the real value directly. As a result, we need an approach to estimate the error between deduced value and real value in each sensing cycle. Moreover, because discrepancy is inevitable in estimation, it is impossible to guarantee the error of all the cells to be less than the predefined bound. Therefore, instead of merely setting the error bound to each cell in each sensing cycle, we need a probabilistic metric to assess data quality.

In the next sections of this chapter, we will see how the above challenges are solved by a framework named *CCS-TA*, which is proposed in [13].

8.2 Problem Statement

Let us first introduce the preliminaries of the problem. In this section, we will first define some key concepts that will be used in problem statement and problem solving. Next, we clarify the assumptions of our solution and formally define the problem.

8.2.1 Definitions

To formally define the sensing quality metric that is used throughout the solution, let us first define the concepts about the *sensing and selection matrices*.

Definition 8.1 (*Full Sensing Matrix*) The full sensing matrix records the true value of the data in the target area (ground truth), which is denoted as $[F(i, j)]_{m \times n}$ for a location-centric MCS task involving m cells and n sensing cycles. Each entry $F(i, j)$ denotes the true sensing data of cell i in cycle j.

Definition 8.2 (*Cell-Selection Matrix*) The Cell-Selection Matrix records which cells are selected to be sensed. It is denoted as $[S(i, j)]_{m \times n}$. If the cell i is selected for sensing in cycle j, $S(i, j) = 1$; otherwise, $S(i, j) = 0$.

Definition 8.3 (*Collected Sensing Matrix*) The Collected Sensing Matrix records the data that is actually collected. It is defined as

$$[C(i, j)]_{m \times n} = F \circ S, \tag{8.1}$$

where the operator $\circ$ denotes the element-wise product of two matrices.

Definition 8.4 (*Sensing Matrix Reconstruction Algorithm*) The Sensing Matrix Reconstruction Algorithm, denoted by $\mathcal{R}(\cdot)$, is a function that deduces the data of unselected cells and reconstruct a approximate Full Sensing Matrix $\hat{F}_{m \times n}$ from Collected Sensing Matrix C:

$$\hat{F}_{m \times n} = \mathcal{R}(C_{m \times n}) \approx F_{m \times n}. \tag{8.2}$$

Next are the definitions representing for data quality:

Definition 8.5 (*Overall Sensing Error*) It quantifies the difference between the reconstructed full sensing matrix $\hat{F}$ and the true full sensing matrix F. We focus on the overall sensing error of each sensing cycle separately. For sensing cycle k, the overall sensing error is defined as

$$\mathcal{E}_k = error(\hat{F}(:, k), F(:, k)), \tag{8.3}$$

where $F(:, k)$ is the kth column of F, i.e., the true sensing values of all the m cells in cycle k, $\hat{F}(:, k)$ contains the corresponding deduced sensing values by using the reconstruction algorithm $mathcal R(\cdot)$, and $error(\cdot)$ function is the specific technique to calculate the overall sensing error. The selection of $error(\cdot)$ function depends on the type of the sensing data. In this chapter, two widely used metrics are used: *mean absolute error* (MAE), which is suitable for continuous value (e.g., temperature [3]), and *classification error*, which is suitable for classification labels (e.g., PM2.5 air quality index (AQI) descriptors [16]):

- *Mean Absolute Error*

$$error(\hat{F}(:, k), F(:, k)) = \frac{\sum_{i=1}^{m} |\hat{F}(i, k) - F(i, k)|}{m}. \tag{8.4}$$

- *Classification Error*

$$error(\hat{F}(:, k), F(:, k)) = 1 - \frac{\sum_{i=1}^{m} I(\psi(\hat{F}(i, k)), \psi(F(i, k)))}{m}, \tag{8.5}$$

where $\psi(\cdot)$ is the function to map a value to its classification label. $I(x, y) = 1$ if $x = y$, otherwise 0.

Definition 8.6 (($\epsilon, p) - quality$) An MCS task satisfies ($\epsilon, p) - quality$ iff.

$$|\{k|\mathcal{E}_k \leq \epsilon, 1 \leq k \leq n\}| \geq n \cdot p, \tag{8.6}$$

where ϵ is the error bound for the overall sensing error in a single sensing cycle, n is the number of sensing cycle of an MCS task, and p is the proportion of the sensing cycles where the overall sensing error should be less than the error bound ϵ.

Ideally, we want the overall sensing error of all sensing cycles are less than the error bound, i.e., $p = 1$. In this case, the $(\epsilon, p) - quality$ becomes $(\epsilon, 1) - quality$. However, it is hard to ensure the $(\epsilon, 1) - quality$ in real-world MCS applications, because the overall sensing error $\mathcal{E}_k$ of a sensing cycle is not known in advance. We have to estimate it with an unknown ground truth F. Thus, we loosen the restriction by letting $p < 1$ but still large enough (e.g., 0.9 or 0.95, etc.). This will guarantee the overall error of most sensing cycles be bounded to ϵ. Furthermore, this will also allow us to take advantage of probability theory and Bayesian statistics to handle the problem. We will show how this works later.

8.2.2 Assumptions

For simplicity, the following assumptions are made.

Assumption 8.1 (*Massive Candidate Participants*) There are sufficient number of candidate participants across the target sensing area, so for any cell in any sensing cycle, the organizer can always find a participant to allocate a sensing task.

The Assumption 8.1 is realistic in most MCS applications. A supporting example is the traffic monitoring application *WAZE* (https://www.waze.com), which has more than 50 million users.

Assumption 8.2 (*High-Quality Sensing*) Every participant returns the accurate sensing value if a task is allocated to him.

The Assumption 8.2 may not be true in most MCS applications, but there are various of quality maintenance approaches, such as the one mentioned in Chap. 5. The low-quality sensing result can be removed by these approaches. Here, we just make the Assumption 8.2 for simplicity and thus, we can focus the problem of task allocation.

Assumption 8.3 (*Not Moving Out During Sensing*) After a participant receives a sensing task in a cell, he will not move out of the cell before the sensing is finished.

The Assumption 8.3 can be true if the sensing period is not too long. This is true in most MCS applications. For example, in a temperature-sensing task, the participant can obtain the ambient temperature with a smartphone within several seconds.

Assumption 8.4 (*Cycle-Length-Satisfying Sequential Sensing*) Each sensing cycle is sufficiently long to collect enough sensing values by sequentially allocating tasks the next task is allocated after the sensing value of the previous task is returned.

If Assumption 8.3 is true, the Assumption 8.4 could also be true. For example, in a temperature monitoring application, if a participant can complete the sensing task within 10 s and assume there are 50 sensing tasks in a cycle, only 500 s are needed to finish a sensing cycle. This is a reasonable-length period.

In summary, these four assumptions are made for the following reasons:

- The Assumption 8.1 reduces the task allocation problem to a *cell-selection* problem.
- The Assumptions 8.2 and 8.3 allow us to just allocate one task to one participant in cell i during cycle j, in order to get the true sensing value of cell i in cycle j.
- The Assumption 8.4 allows us to conduct an iterative process where cells are progressively selected for sensing in each cycle.

8.2.3 Problem Formulation

Based on the above definitions and assumptions, the problem can be formulated as following:

Given an MCS task with m cells and n cycles, and a sensing matrix reconstruction algorithm $\mathcal{R}$, select a minimal subset of sensing cells during the whole MCS task process (i.e., minimize the number of nonzero entries in the cell-selection matrix S), while ensuring that the overall sensing errors of at least $n \cdot p$ cycles are below the predefined error bound ϵ (i.e., satisfying the $(\epsilon, p) - quality$):

$$\min \ \sum_{i=1}^{m} \sum_{j=1}^{n} S[i, j]$$
$$\text{s.t.} \ \ |\{k | \mathcal{E}_k \leq \epsilon, 1 \leq k \leq n\}| \geq n \cdot p, \tag{8.7}$$

where

$$\mathcal{E}_k = error(\hat{F}[:, k], F[:, k]), \tag{8.8}$$
$$\hat{F} = \mathcal{R}(C), C = F \circ S. \tag{8.9}$$

This problem is challenging for the following reasons:

1. Because the ground truth F is not known in advance, the overall error $\mathcal{E}_k$ in each sensing cycles cannot be directly obtained.
2. Only after we set $S[i, j] = 1$ can we get $F[i, j]$, and this process cannot be retrieved to reduce the cost of task allocation (we conclude this feature as the *monotonicity* of cell selection.)

To tackle these challenges, in the following sections, we will introduce CCS-TA proposed by [13], in which an iterative process is conducted for cell selection in each sensing cycle.

8.3   Compressive Crowdsensing

In this section, we will describe the CCS-TA solution in detail.

8.3.1   Overview

First, let us browse the CCS-TA solution from an overall perspective. Figure 8.1 shows the conceptional workflow of CCS-TA. In each sensing cycle, the following steps are conducted iteratively: (1) Select a *salient cell* (we should be able to best deduce the value of other cells by obtaining the information of the *salient cell*), and allocate the sensing task to a participant in the selected cell. (2) Assess the task quality by judging if it satisfies the $(\epsilon, p) - quality$. If it is not satisfied, return step (1); else, proceed to step (3). (3) Deduce the missing values in the unselected cells, and stop allocating tasks in the sensing cycle.

Figure 8.2 illustrates a simple example of CCS-TA process with five cells and five cycles. Now, we are at the start of cycle 5. The task allocation process of cycle 5 is as follows:

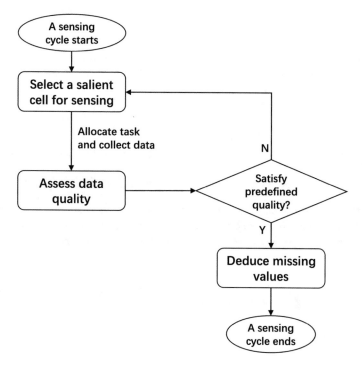

Fig. 8.1 Workflow of CCS-TA

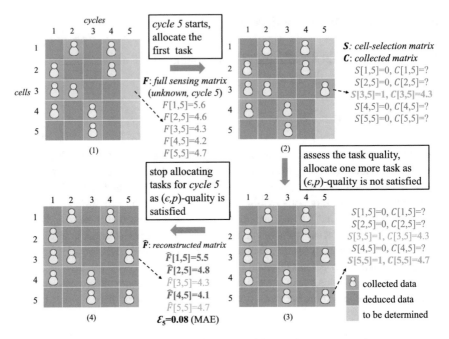

Fig. 8.2 An example of CCS-TA process (five cells and five cycles, temperature)

1. Initially, we have absolutely no idea of the ground truth F. We select a *salient cell* and allocate the first task to a participant in the selected cell. In this example, cell 3 is the selected *salient cell*.
2. Assess the task quality. We find that the $(\epsilon, p) - quality$ is not satisfied, so select one more *salient cell* (in this example, cell 5 is selected) and allocate the task in it to another participant.
3. Assess the task quality again. This time, the $(\epsilon, p) - quality$ is satisfied, so stop allocating the task.
4. Deduce the values in the unselected cells (cell 1, 2, and 4 in this example).

From the workflow and the example, we know that there are three key steps in CCS-TA: *Selecting salient cell for sensing, deducing missing values*, and *determining task allocation stopping criterion*. Next, we will discuss them one by one.

8.3.2   Selecting Salient Cell for Sensing

8.3.2.1   Salient Cell

At the start of a sensing cycle or when $(\epsilon, p) - quality$ is not satisfied, we will need to select a new cell for sensing. The selected cell is called *salient cell*, which is defined as *the cell that can help the value in the unselected cells to the maximum extent*. The selection of the *salient cell* is based on the following intuition: among all the unselected cells, the value of some cells may be more uncertain and thus is more difficult to deduce. If we can identify these cells as *salient cells*, the number of the selected cells needed to guarantee the $(\epsilon, p) - quality$ may be minimized.

8.3.2.2 Query by Committee

Based on the recent researches in *active learning*, a method proposed in [5] is applied, which is called *Query by Committee (QBC)*, to select the *salient cell* for the next iteration of sensing. In QBC, a series of data reconstruction algorithms are selected to form a *committee* and the values of the unselected cells are deduced by each algorithm in the *committee* respectively. Among the deduced result of all algorithms, the cell with the largest variance is selected as the *salient cell* and the sensing task of the next iteration will be allocated in it.

In CCS-TA, the member of the committee includes *CS, STCS, KNN-S* and *KNN-T*. Among them, *CS* and *STCS* are Compressive Sensing and Spatial–Temporal Compressive Sensing, which are similar to that in Sects. 4.3.2 and 4.5. *KNN-S* and *KNN-T* are based on the classical *K-Nearest Neighbors (KNN)*. For a missing value, *KNN* deduce it as the weighted average of the values of its k nearest neighbors. In the context of matrix completion, we can either apply *KNN* on *columns* or on *rows*, i.e., either in spatial dimension (*KNN-S*) or in temporal dimension (*KNN-T*).

8.3.2.3 Computational Complexity of QBC

The running time of *QBC* is basically determined by the computational complexity of each data reconstruct algorithm in the *committee*. Suppose for each data reconstruct algorithm $\mathcal{R}_i$ in the *committee*, the computational complexity is $T_{\mathcal{R}_i}$, the overall computational complexity of *QBC* is $\sum_i T_{\mathcal{R}_i}$. Generally speaking, if the algorithms in the *committee* are conducted in sequence, the running time will increase linearly with the growth of the number of the algorithms in the *committee*. Fortunately, because the process of each algorithm is independent, the running time can be optimized by conducting the data reconstruct algorithms in parallel.

8.3.3 Deducing Missing Values

Another key step in CCS-TA is deducing the missing values in the unselected cells. The deduction of missing values is not only conducted when the task allocation iteration ends (see Fig. 8.1), but also in each iteration of the task allocation when determining task allocation stopping criterion.

In this chapter, the *Spatiotemporal Compressive Sensing (STCS)* is selected as the data reconstruction method to deduce the unknown values. The selected *STCS* algorithm is similar to the *ESTI-CS* introduced in Sect. 4.5. The final form of the compressive sensing problem is as follows:

$$\min \|S \circ (LR^T) - C\|_F^2 + \lambda(\|L\|_F^2 + \|R\|_F^2) + \|LR^T \mathbb{T}\|_F^2 + \|\mathbb{H}LR^T\|_F^2, \quad (8.10)$$

where $\mathbb{T}$ and $\mathbb{H}$ are *temporal constraint matrix* and *spatial constraint matrix* defined in Sect. 4.5. The readers can refer to Sect. 4.5 for more detail.

8.3.4 Stopping Criterion for Task Allocation

In each sensing cycle of CCS-TA, how to decide if the sensing iteration should be terminated? This is another key issue in the design of CCS-TA. Apparently, the iteration should not be terminated too early, or the predefined $(\epsilon, p) - quality$ may not be satisfied, and thus the deduced data may be in poor quality. The iteration process should also not be terminated too late. If so, the efficiency of task allocation may be deteriorated because more tasks than needed are allocated and thus the cost of employing participants and the length of each sensing cycle may increase. A well-designed stopping criterion should guarantee the data quality to satisfy the $(\epsilon, p) - quality$, while minimizing the rounds of iteration in each sensing cycle (i.e., the number of the selected *salient cells* and allocated tasks should be minimized).

To achieve this, a *Leave-One-Out Bayesian-Inference (LOO-BI)*-based method is designed. *LOO-BI* is comprised of two steps: *Leave-One-Out Re-Sampling* and *Bayesian Inference*. As depicted in Algorithm 8.1, the *Leave-One-Out Re-Sampling* method try to deduce the value of collected data and compare the re-deduced data with the true value of them. Next, the *Bayesian Inference* is conducted to judge if the current quality of the collected data and the deduced data satisfies with the predefined $(\epsilon, p) - quality$.

Next, we will introduce the two parts, respectively.

8.3.4.1 Leave-One-Out Re-Sampling

Leave-one-out is a popular re-sampling method to assess the performance of prediction problems. It has been widely used in machine learning area. The principle of this method is as following: Suppose we have m true values (as ground truth), we manually select $(m - 1)$ values among them and make prediction to the excluded value. This process is conducted over all m values and finally, we get m predicted values. The performance of the prediction algorithm can be assessed according to the difference of the m predicted values and m true values.

Algorithm 8.1: LOO-BI task allocation stopping criterion

Input : $C_{m \times k}$: collected sensing matrix with m locations and k cycles;
$\mathcal{R}()$: a sensing matrix reconstruction algorithm;
error: an error matrix;
ϵ, p: predefined $(\epsilon, p) - quality$ requirement.

Output: *stop*: a boolean value determining whether stop or continue task allocation.

1 $\mathbf{x} \leftarrow []$;
2 $\mathbf{y} \leftarrow []$;
3 **for** $i \leftarrow 1$ *to* m **do**
4   **if** $C[i, k] \neq null$ **then**
5      $\mathbf{x}.append(C[i, k])$;
6      $C' \leftarrow C$;
7      $C'[i, k] \leftarrow null$;
8      $\hat{F}' \leftarrow \mathcal{R}(C')$;
9      $\mathbf{y}.append(\hat{F}'[i, k])$;

10 $P(\mathcal{E}_k \leq \epsilon) \leftarrow BayesianInference(error, \mathbf{x}, \mathbf{y}, \epsilon)$;
11 **if** $P(\mathcal{E}_k \leq \epsilon)$ **then**
12    $stop \leftarrow true$;

13 **else**
14    $stop \leftarrow false$;

15 **return** $stop$;

The basic idea of the Leave-one-out method is applied to the data of current sensing cycle (the kth cycle) in the first part of Algorithm 8.1 (before line 12). In Algorithm 8.1, $\mathbf{x}$ is the vector of collected data and $\mathbf{y}$ is the vector of the deduced data. Different to traditional leave-one-out method, in each round of re-sampling, the excluded data is deduced based on not only the collected data of current sensing cycle, but also the collected and deduced data of the previous sensing cycles.

Suppose we have already collected data for m' cells in the current sensing cycle, then after leave-one-out re-sampling, the vector $\mathbf{x}$ and $\mathbf{y}$ would be:

$$\mathbf{x} = < x_1, x_2, \ldots, x_{m'} >, \mathbf{y} = < y_1, y_2, \ldots, y_{m'} >, \tag{8.11}$$

where x_i is the true value of the data in the ith cell and y_i is the deduced value of x_i by leaving x_i out of the collected data.

Based on the true value of the collected data $\mathbf{x}$ and the re-deduced data $\mathbf{y}$, we will leverage the Bayesian Inference to judge if the collected data and the deduced values based on it could satisfy the $(\epsilon, p) - quality$.

8.3.4.2 Assessing Task Quality by Bayesian Inference

According to *the law of large numbers* [7], the $(\epsilon, p) - quality$ can be converted into the following probability form:

$$\forall k, 1 \leq k \leq n : P(\mathcal{E}_k \leq \epsilon) \geq p. \tag{8.12}$$

Thus, we can assess if the $(\epsilon, p) - quality$ is satisfied by simply calculating the probability $P(\mathcal{E}_k \leq \epsilon)$, which can be easily obtained if the probability distribution of $\mathcal{E}_k$ is known. Now the problem becomes, how can we know the probability distribution of $\mathcal{E}_k$? This can be achieved via Bayesian inference [8].

In Bayesian inference, $\mathcal{E}_k$ is considered as a random variable with a *prior* probability distribution $g(\mathcal{E}_k)$. Next, the distribution of $\mathcal{E}_k$ is updated based on our observation θ, which is calculated from the true value $\mathbf{x}$ and the re-deduced data $\mathbf{y}$. The relationship between $\mathbf{x}$, $\mathbf{y}$ and θ is specific to applications. We will show two examples later. The updated probability distribution is called the *posterior* probability distribution and noted as $g(\mathcal{E}_k|\theta)$. The update process is conducted according to the *Bayes' Theorem*:

$$g(\mathcal{E}_k|\theta) = \frac{f(\theta|\mathcal{E}_k)g(\mathcal{E}_k)}{\int_{-\infty}^{+\infty} f(\theta|\mathcal{E}_k)g(\mathcal{E}_k)d\mathcal{E}_k}, \tag{8.13}$$

where $f(\theta|\mathcal{E}_k)$ is the likelihood function representing the probability of observing θ given $\mathcal{E}_k$.

The posterior distribution $g(\mathcal{E}_k|\theta)$ is considered as the approximation of the true distribution of $\mathcal{E}_k$. Then, the probability $P(\mathcal{E}_k$ can be calculated as

$$P(\mathcal{E}_k) \approx \int_{-\infty}^{\epsilon} g(\mathcal{E}_k|\theta)d\mathcal{E}_k. \tag{8.14}$$

If $P(\mathcal{E}_k) > p$, we can assert that the $(\epsilon, p) - quality$ has been satisfied and the current sensing cycle ends. Otherwise, it suggests the $(\epsilon, p) - quality$ has not been satisfied and a new cell is selected for sensing data.

It is worth noting that for different applications and error metrics, the calculation process for the posterior $g(\mathcal{E}_k|\theta)$ differs, because the calculation of θ and the likelihood function $f(\theta|\mathcal{E}_k)$ are different. Next, we will show two examples in which the posterior distribution of *mean absolute error* (MAE) and *classification error* are calculated, respectively.

8.3.4.3 Bayesian Inference for Mean Absolute Error

When the overall error $\mathcal{E}_k$ is defined as MAE, the observation θ is calculated as the absolute difference between the true value $\mathbf{x}$ and the re-deduced data $\mathbf{y}$. Suppose values of m' cells have been collected in the current cycle, θ can be represented as

$$\theta = < |y_1 - x_1|, |y_2 - x_2|, \ldots, |y_{m'} - x_{m'}| > . \tag{8.15}$$

Through experiment, we find that the MAE in each sensing cycle follows the normal distribution. Suppose the mean is $\mathcal{E}_k$ and the variance is σ^2, the likelihood function can be represented as

$$f(\theta|\mathcal{E}_k) : \theta_i = |y_i - x_i| \sim \mathcal{N}(\mathcal{E}_k, \sigma^2). \tag{8.16}$$

Now, calculating the posterior $g(\mathcal{E}_k|\theta)$ is equivalent to inferring normal mean with unknown variance, which is a classic Bayesian statistic problem and can be solved by assuming the the the variance σ^2 as the sample variance s^2 and leveraging the t-distribution [4]. The *Jeffreys' flat prior* [10] is selected: $g(\mathcal{E}_k) = 1, \forall k$. Then, the posterior $g(\mathcal{E}_k|\theta)$ satisfies the following $(m'-1)$ degree of freedom t-distribution:

$$g(\mathcal{E}_k|\theta) \sim t_{m'-1}(\bar{\theta}, s^2), \tag{8.17}$$

where $\bar{\theta}$ is the mean of the values in θ.

8.3.4.4 Bayesian Inference for Classification Error

For classification problems, the overall error $\mathcal{E}_k$ is defined as classification error (Eq. 8.5), which measures the percentage of the test data that is classified into a wrong label. The process of calculating the posterior distribution $g(\mathcal{E}_k|\theta)$ is as following:

First, we need to map the continuous value in $\mathbf{x}$ and $\mathbf{y}$ into their corresponding classification labels using the mapping function $\psi()$ in Eq. 8.5. As an example, Table 8.1 shows a typical mapping function in a air quality monitoring application. For the AQI values between 0 and 50, the function $\psi()$ map them as *Good*; those between 50 and 100 are mapped as *Moderate*, etc.. After that, *identity function* $I()$ is applied on $\psi(\mathbf{x})$ and $\psi(\mathbf{y})$ to calculate the observation θ:

$$\theta = I(\psi(\mathbf{x}), \psi(\mathbf{y})) \tag{8.18}$$
$$= < I(\psi(x_1), \psi(y_1)), I(\psi(x_2), \psi(y_2)), \dots, I(\psi(x_{m'}), \psi(y_{m'})) >. \tag{8.19}$$

Each θ_i is either 1 (when $\psi(x_i) = \psi(y_i)$) or 0 (when $\psi(x_i) \neq \psi(y_i)$), and the overall error $\mathcal{E}_k$ is the failure ratio. Suppose each θ_i is independent, then it satisfies the *Bernoulli distribution* with the probability of $1 - \mathcal{E}_k$):

$$f(\theta|\mathcal{E}_k) : \theta_i = I(\psi(x_i), \psi(y_i)) \sim Bernoulli(1 - \mathcal{E}_k). \tag{8.20}$$

Based on this likelihood function $f(\theta|\mathcal{E}_k)$, the problem to infer the posterior distribution $g(\mathcal{E}_k|\theta)$ can be converted to a classic Bayesian statistics problem, *Coin Flipping* [4, 8]. The uniform prior is chosen for $\mathcal{E}_k : g(\mathcal{E}_k) = 1$ for $0 \leq \mathcal{E}_k \leq 1$. Then the posterior for $\mathcal{E}_k$ follows Beta distribution [4, 8]:

$$g(\mathcal{E}_k|\theta) \sim Beta(m' - z + 1, z + 1), \tag{8.21}$$

where $z = \sum_{i=1}^{m'} \theta_i$ is the the number of successes ($\psi(x_i) = \psi(y_i)$).

8.3.4.5 Computational Complexity of LOO-BI

There are two steps in LOO-BI—leave-one-out re-sampling and Bayesian inference. In the leave-one-out re-sampling step, the reconstruction algorithm needs to be executed for m' times, where m' is the number of cells that have been allocated as sensing cells in the current sensing cycle. Suppose the computational complexity is $T_{\mathcal{R}}$, then the overall computational complexity of the leave-one-out step is $O(m' \cdot T_{\mathcal{R}})$. In the Bayesian-inference step, we just need to calculate the observation θ and calculate the integration of a t-distribution or $Beta$ distribution to estimate the probability $P(\mathcal{E}_k \leq \epsilon)$. The computational complexity is constant $O(1)$. Combine these two parts, the overall computational complexity of LOO-BI is $O(m' \cdot T_{\mathcal{R}})$. In addition, as the execution of the m' reconstruction algorithms are independent, the process can be accelerated by parallelizing the execution of the m' reconstruction algorithms.

8.4 Evaluation

In this section, we will have a brief review of the evaluation of CCS-TA. The readers can refer to [13] for the detailed result of the evaluation.

8.4.1 Experiment Setup

The evaluation is based on two real-world data sets—*temperature (TEMP)* and *PM 2.5 air quality (PM25)*. It is worth noting that these two data sets are collected via wireless sensor network, while we assume that they are obtained by MCS participants using their smartphones.

The *TEMP* data set has been collected by the *SensorScope* project [1]. The project collects environmental information including temperature across an area of 500 m × 300 m in the EPFL campus. In the evaluation, the area is divided into 100 cells and temperature is obtained from 57 among them. In summary, the *TEMP* data set is comprised of the temperature readings from 57 cells from July 7, 2007 to July 7, 2007, with a sensing cycle of 30 min. The Mean Absolute Error (MAE) metric is used to assess the data quality of the temperature.

The *PM25* data set has been collected by the *U-Air* project [16], in which PM2.5 values is reported by 36 air quality monitoring stations in Beijing. In the evaluation, the Beijing urban area is divided into 1 km × 1 km cells and only those contain

Table 8.1 Mapping function of the $PM2.5$ AQI

AQI range	Air quality condition
0–50	Good
51–100	Moderate
101–150	Unhealthy for sensitive groups
151–200	Unhealthy
201–300	Very unhealthy
>301	Hazardous

an air quality monitoring station are used. In summary, the *PM25* data set includes the $PM2.5$ AQI values on 36 station-situated cells from November 10, 2013 to November 20, 2013, whit a sensing cycle of 60 min. The data quality is assessed by the classification error, and the mapping function $\psi()$ is shown as Table 8.1.

8.4.2 Performance Analysis

In this book, we inspect the performance of CCS-TA mainly from two aspects: *number of allocated tasks* and *running time*. The readers can refer to [13] for more detailed performance evaluation results.

8.4.2.1 Number of Allocated Tasks

To evaluate the number of allocated tasks in CCS-TA, we take the following baselines as comparison:

- *ICDM-FIX-k*: An alternative way to extend the *QBC* active learning method [5] to the MCS task allocation mechanism is fixing the task number k in each sensing cycle, while still using *QBC* to actively select cells to allocate tasks.
- *RAND-TA*: In this baseline, the next cell for sensing is randomly selected, while still leverage *LOO-BI* as the task allocation stopping criterion.

The evaluation result is summarized in Tables 8.2 and 8.3. For the *TEMP* data set (Table 8.2), the error bound ϵ is set as 0.25 °C, and the p varies from 0.9 to 0.95. We observe that when $p = 0.9$, the average number of allocated tasks of *CCS-TA* is about 7.3, which is 0.9 and 1.7 fewer than that of *RAND-TA* and *ICDM-FIX-k*. When $p = 0.95$, the average number of allocated tasks of *CCS-TA* is 8.9, which is 0.8 and 3.1 fewer than that of *RAND-TA* and *ICDM-FIX-k*, respectively. For the *PM25* data set (Table 8.3), the error bound ϵ is set as 9/36 (i.e., 0.25), and the p also varies from 0.9 to 0.95. When $p = 0.9$, the average number of allocated tasks of *CCS-TA* is about 11.0, which is 1.1 and 4.8 fewer than that of *RAND-TA* and *ICDM-FIX-k*.

Table 8.2 Number of allocated tasks (TEMP, $\epsilon = 0.25\,°C$, varying p)

TEMP	CCS-TA	RAND-TA	ICDM-FIX-k
$p = 0.9$	7.3	8.2	9.0
$p = 0.95$	8.9	10.7	12.0

Table 8.3 Number of allocated tasks (PM25, $\epsilon = 9/36$, varying p)

PM25	CCS-TA	RAND-TA	ICDM-FIX-k
$p = 0.9$	11.0	12.1	15.8
$p = 0.95$	13.5	14.7	18.0

Table 8.4 Running time for each sub-step of CCS-TA

	Reconstruction (STCS) (s)	Stopping criterion (LOO-BI) (s)	Cell selection (QBC) (s)
TEMP	0.95	<9	1.04
PM25	0.75	<7	0.91

When $p = 0.95$, the average number of allocated tasks of *CCS-TA* is 13.5, which is 1.2 and 4.5 fewer than that of *RAND-TA* and *ICDM-FIX-k*, respectively.

8.4.2.2   Running Time

The running time is evaluated to test if the CCS-TA is feasible in real-world scenario. The experiment is conducted on a laptop (Intel Core i7-3612QM, 8GB RAM, Windows 7) with Python 2.7. Table 8.4 summarizes the running time needed for a single task allocation. From the result, we observe that the most time-consuming part in CCS-TA is the *LOO-BI* step, which contains multiple reconstruction processes. The *LOO-BI* and *QBC* steps can be further optimized via parallelism, as discussed in Sects. 8.3.2 and 8.3.4. In summary, under the experiment setup, CCS-TA is able to allocate one task within about 10 s, and the task allocation process continues until the $(\epsilon, p) - quality$ is fulfilled. Suppose the participant need t_0 seconds to collect a single value, the CCS-TA is able to allocate about $3600/(t_0 + 10)$ tasks in an hour. In the temperature sensing scenario where the participant needs only 10 s to get a valid value, the CCS-TA is able to allocate about $3600/(10 + 10) = 180$ tasks in an hour. This should be efficient enough for real-world MCS applications.

8.5 Summary

In this chapter, we first raised the idea of Compressive Crowdsensing (CCS). In CCS, instead of obtaining information from all around the target area, only a subset of the target area is selected as sample, and the information of the unselected area can be deduced from the value of selected area. The main problem in CCS is task allocation problem, which is twofold: How large should the size of the sampled area be, and how to judge which part of the area should be sampled. To solve this problem, we introduced a framework named *CCS-TA*, which combines compressive sensing, Bayesian inference, and an active learning process to actively select a minimum subset of the target area for sensing, while guarantees the overall data quality satisfies to the $(\epsilon, p) - quality$. The evaluation based on a temperature data set and a PM2.5 data set showed that *CCS-TA* can achieve relatively less allocated task number within a reasonable time limit.

References

1. (2007) Shtc1-digital temperature and humidity sensor. http://www.sensirion.com/en/products/humidity-temperature/humidity-temperature-sensor-shtc1/. Accessed 24 June 2015
2. Ahmed A, Yasumoto K, Yamauchi Y, Ito M (2011) Distance and time based node selection for probabilistic coverage in people-centric sensing. In: 2011 8th annual IEEE communications society conference on sensor, mesh and ad hoc communications and networks (SECON). IEEE, pp 134–142
3. Bolstad PV, Swift L, Collins F, Régnière J (1998) Measured and predicted air temperatures at basin to regional scales in the southern Appalachian mountains. Agric For Meteorol 91(3–4):161–176
4. Bolstad WM, Curran JM (2016) Introduction to Bayesian statistics. Wiley
5. Chakraborty S, Zhou J, Balasubramanian V, Panchanathan S, Davidson I, Ye J (2013) Active matrix completion. In: International conference on data mining (ICDM). IEEE, pp 81–90
6. Chon Y, Lane ND, Kim Y, Zhao F, Cha H (2013) Understanding the coverage and scalability of place-centric crowdsensing. In: International joint conference on pervasive and ubiquitous computing (Ubicomp). ACM, pp 3–12
7. Feller W (2008) An introduction to probability theory and its applications, vol 2. Wiley
8. Gelman A, Stern HS, Carlin JB, Dunson DB, Vehtari A, Rubin DB (2013) Bayesian data analysis. Chapman and Hall/CRC
9. Hachem S, Pathak A, Issarny V (2013) Probabilistic registration for large-scale mobile participatory sensing. In: International conference on pervasive computing and communications (PerCom). IEEE, pp 132–140
10. Jeffreys H (1946) An invariant form for the prior probability in estimation problems. Proc R Soc Lond Ser A Math Phys Sci 186(1007):453–461
11. Li H, Li T, Wang W, Wang Y (2018) Dynamic participant selection for large-scale mobile crowd sensing. IEEE Trans Mob Comput
12. Sheng X, Tang J, Zhang W (2012) Energy-efficient collaborative sensing with mobile phones. In: International conference on computer communications (INFOCOM). IEEE, pp 1916–1924
13. Wang L, Zhang D, Pathak A, Chen C, Xiong H, Yang D, Wang Y (2015) CCS-TA: quality-guaranteed online task allocation in compressive crowdsensing. In: International joint conference on pervasive and ubiquitous computing (Ubicomp). ACM, pp 683–694

14. Xiong H, Zhang D, Wang L, Chaouchi H (2015) Emc 3: energy-efficient data transfer in mobile crowdsensing under full coverage constraint. IEEE Trans Mob Comput (TMC) 14(7):1355–1368
15. Zhang D, Xiong H, Wang L, Chen G (2014) Crowdrecruiter: selecting participants for piggyback crowdsensing under probabilistic coverage constraint. In: International joint conference on pervasive and ubiquitous computing (Ubicomp). ACM, pp 703–714
16. Zheng Y, Liu F, Hsieh HP (2013) U-air: when urban air quality inference meets big data. In: International conference on knowledge discovery and data mining (SIGKDD). ACM, pp 1436–1444

Chapter 9
Conclusion

In this book, we have studied the systematic compressive sensing- based solution to solve the data quality problem in mobile crowdsensing.

In Chap. 1, we introduced the concept of mobile crowdsensing and compressive sensing. On one hand, mobile crowdsensing is a promising paradigm to collect environment information by mobilizing the crowd to participate in the data collection tasks. Compared to traditional data obtaining method, mobile crowdsensing is more efficient, easier to implement, and low-cost. However, as a relatively new technique, crowdsensing is encountered with the data quality problem, including missing data, faulty data, privacy-preserving, multidimensional data, and task allocation. On the other hand, compressive sensing is a new technique to discover the intrinsic property of data, compress data and reconstruct data. It can be utilized to facilitate the development of mobile crowdsensing.

In Chap. 2, we briefly introduced the structure of mobile crowdsensing. Especially, we stated the data quality problem. This problem has attracted many research works. We comprehensively discuss the existing solutions from six categories. We found that existing solutions are based on various theoretical foundations, which may exist in compatibility problem. Hence, we recommend the systematic solution based on compressive sensing.

In Chap. 3, we took a review of the principle of compressive sensing. We first introduced the concept of *sparse* of vectors, and then showed that the sparse signals are compressible and can be recovered accurately. Next, we extended the concept of *sparse* to matrices and derived the basic form of matrix completion in compressive sensing. Finally, we formulated the basic form of data reconstruction problem of compressive sensing. These basic forms will be utilized in the following chapters and be solved by different procedure, according to different applications.

Chapter 4 shows the first application where the basic compressive sensing is utilized in mobile crowdsensing. The application in this chapter focuses on missing data in Mobile Crowdsensing. This is an excellent example of showing how powerful compressive sensing is in data reconstruction. With principal component

© Springer Nature Singapore Pte Ltd. 2019
L. Kong et al., *When Compressive Sensing Meets Mobile Crowdsensing*, https://doi.org/10.1007/978-981-13-7776-1_9

analysis, we have analyzed a large data set of real probe data collected from a fleet of 4,000 taxis in Shanghai, China, and discover that road traffic condition matrices often embody hidden structures or redundancy. Inspired by this observation, we have designed the algorithm based on compressive sensing, which effectively exploits the internal structures of traffic condition matrices. Experiments with the large data set of probe data have verified that the algorithm significantly outperforms other competing algorithms, including two variations of KNN and MSSA. At last, we briefly introduce how to further improve the accuracy of compressive sensing by utilizing temporal and spatial correlations in the data.

On the basis of Chap. 4, in Chap. 5 we further took faulty data into consideration. In this scenario, both missing data and faulty data are presented in the dataset. The present of faulty data hinders the application of compressive sensing, because compressive sensing is not tolerant to faulty data. To address this problem, we introduced a framework called iterative compressive sensing, in which time series-based outlier detection method and compressive sensing is iteratively conducted.

With the increasing popularity of location-based services, it is important to simultaneously consider the quality of service and user privacy. In Chap. 6, we studied the problem of privacy-preserving during data reconstruction. We introduced a novel homogeneous compressive sensing scheme, which uses compressive sensing to accurately recover the trajectories with the consideration of privacy. The core design of homogeneous compressive sensing scheme leverages the matrix transformation to encrypt the data while guarantee the homogeneous proper include the privacy preservation into compressive sensing.

In Chap. 7, we focused on user-provided information in mobile crowdsensing. Unlike the data discussed in the previous chapters, user-provided information describes complicated phenomenons and is multidimensional. This hinders the direct application of compressive sensing. To address this problem, we introduced a *converted compressive sensing* framework, which is able to convert the data structure of the original data into a form that is suitable for compressive sensing. Moreover, the converted compressive sensing also conducts *base training* on the historical data in order to accurately capture the sparse property of specific type of data. Finally, the converted compressive sensing adopts *Orthogonal Matching Pursuit* to solve the compressive sensing problem.

In Chap. 8, we considered another scenario, where compressive sensing was applied when the data is being collected. Instead of passively recovering the incomplete dataset after the data had been collected, in Chap. 6, we actively reduced the size of the allocated tasks to reduce the cost. This is realized by Compressive Crowdsensing (*CCS*). In *CCS*, instead of obtaining information from all around the target area, only a subset of the target area is selected as sample, and the information of the unselected area can be deduced from the value of selected area. The main problem in *CCS* is task allocation problem, which is twofold: How large should the size of the sampled area be, and how to judge which part of the area should be sampled. To solve this problem, we introduced a framework named *CCS-TA*, which combines compressive sensing, Bayesian inference, and an active learning process to actively select a minimum subset of the target area for sensing, while guarantees the overall data quality.

We believe compressive sensing has wider implications for mobile crowdsensing than explored in this book. The promising future directions include but not limited by

- *Time Complexity Optimization*: Although there are various approaches to solve the compressive sensing problem, most of them are computationally intensive. This is because each iteration of these algorithms contains several matrix multiplication operations, resulting in a time complexity up to $O(n^3)$ (suppose the sizes of both matrices are $n \times n$. If the size of the matrix is large, the time needed would be considerable. In order to improve the efficiency of compressive sensing based data quality management, the time complexity is desired to be optimized.
- *Offline and Online Collaboration*: The frameworks introduced in Chaps. 4, 5 and 6 all run offline. However, in practice, most applications require real-time data management. It would be valuable to enable these algorithms to run online. Distributed computing in edge devices is a potential solution.
- *Multiple Variables Correlation*: All solutions introduced in this book focus on only one type of variable (e.g., location, temperature or AQI, etc.). However, in practice, MCS applications usually collect multiple variables. Correlations might exist between these variables. Discovering and utilize these correlations may further improve the data quality.
- *Non-numerical Data Management*: The frameworks introduced in Chap. 4 to Chap. 8 are all designed for numerical values, e.g., location, sensor readings, etc. Nevertheless, non-numerical data are inevitable in some MCS applications, e.g., health condition report, survey response, etc. Although user-provided information is considered in Chap. 7, the actual data processed by compressive sensing is the frequency of each result, which is still numerical. It is valuable to extend the compressive sensing algorithm to non-numerical data in the future.

Printed in the United States
By Bookmasters